EXERCISES AND MANŒUVRES
OF
THE LANCE

by

Lieut.-Colonel Reymond Hervey De Montmorency

The Naval & Military Press Ltd

published in association with

ROYAL
ARMOURIES

Published by
The Naval & Military Press Ltd
Unit 10 Ridgewood Industrial Park,
Uckfield, East Sussex,
TN22 5QE England
Tel: +44 (0) 1825 749494
Fax: +44 (0) 1825 765701
www.naval-military-press.com

in association with

ROYAL
ARMOURIES

*In reprinting in facsimile from the original, any imperfections are inevitably reproduced
and the quality may fall short of modern type and cartographic standards.*

Printed and bound by Antony Rowe Ltd, Eastbourne

Prince Joseph Poniatowski.

PROPOSED RULES AND REGULATIONS

FOR THE

EXERCISE AND MANŒUVRES

OF

THE LANCE,

COMPILED ENTIRELY FROM THE POLISH SYSTEM, INSTITUTED BY
MARSHAL PRINCE JOSEPH PONIATOWSKI;
AND GENERAL COUNT CORVIN KRASINSKI,

AND ADAPTED TO

𝕿𝖍𝖊 𝕱𝖔𝖗𝖒𝖆𝖙𝖎𝖔𝖓𝖘, 𝕸𝖔𝖛𝖊𝖒𝖊𝖓𝖙𝖘, 𝖆𝖓𝖉 𝕰𝖝𝖊𝖗𝖈𝖎𝖘𝖊

OF THE

BRITISH CAVALRY.

TO WHICH IS AFFIXED,

AN HISTORICAL ACCOUNT OF THE MOST CELEBRATED BANNERS AND ORDERS OF
CHIVALRY, BEING EMBLEMATIC AND DESCRIPTIVE OF THE ORIGIN AND
HONOR FORMERLY ATTACHED TO BEARING GONFANONS, OR
GONFALONS, CHIVALRIC BANNERS, AND LANCES.

BY LIEUT. COLONEL REYMOND HERVEY DE MONTMORENCY,

H. P. YORK HUSSARS,

LATE LIEUTENANT COLONEL AND MAJOR IN HIS MAJESTY'S 9TH LANCERS.

" By Jove, I am not covetous for gold ;
Nor care I who doth feed upon my cost ;
It yearns me not if men my garments wear ;
Such outward things dwell not in my desires :
But, if it be a sin to covet honour,
I am the most offending soul alive."

SHAKESPEARE.

LONDON :

PRINTED FOR LONGMAN, HURST, REES, ORME, AND BROWNE, PATERNOSTER-ROW ;
T. EGERTON, MILITARY LIBRARY, WHITEHALL ;
AND JOHN CUMMING, NO. 16, LOWER ORMOND-QUAY, DUBLIN.

1820.

Palmam qui meruit, ferat.

"Has ego versiculos feci, tulit alter honores.

Sic vos non vobis nidificatis aves.

Sic vos non vobis vellera fertis oves.

Sic vos non vobis mellificatis apes.

Sic vos non vobis fertis aratra boves."

Virgilius in Bathyllum.

TO

FIELD MARSHAL,

His Royal Highness,

FREDERICK DUKE OF YORK, K. G. & G. C. B.

COMMANDER IN CHIEF OF HIS MAJESTY'S FORCES,

&c. &c. &c. &c.

———————

SIR,

IN presenting YOUR ROYAL HIGHNESS with the following Treatise for the Exercise and Manœuvres of the Lance, I am induced to hope that my motive will receive YOUR ROYAL HIGHNESS'S sanction. Many hours of my captivity in France were solaced by the reflection, that, on my return home, my labours would receive the approbation of YOUR ROYAL HIGHNESS, whose gracious protection has been always afforded to those individuals, who, like myself, have aimed at rendering a benefit to that Army, which, under the auspices and regulations of YOUR ROYAL HIGHNESS, has been brought to its present unrivalled state of discipline and renown.

I have the Honor to be,

Sir,

With the most profound Respect,

YOUR ROYAL HIGHNESS'S

Most obedient, and most devoted humble Servant,

REYMOND HERVEY DE MONTMORENCY,

LIEUT. COLONEL H. P. YORK HUSSARS.

LONDON, 25th JUNE, 1820.

PREFACE.

THE Lance was originally the most distinguished of arms, and the most ancient in Europe: in the Cavalry, none but persons of exalted rank and distinction were entitled to be armed with Lances. Henry the Third of France, by an edict, A. D. 1575, decreed, that those who bore Lances were to be selected from among the nobility alone. Lances were denominated, in the ancient Chapters, "*Arma Patriæ*," "*National Arms*." Kings, Princes, Nobles, and Knights, regarded the Lance as the most honorable arm, disdaining all others, except the Sword.

The Lance is composed of the Spear, Plate 1, Fig. 1. The Socket of the Spear, Fig. 2. The Ball of the Spear, Fig. 3. The great Bandlet, Fig. 4. The counter Bandlet, Fig. 5. The Shaft, Fig. 6. The Socket of the Butt, or Ferrule, Fig. 7. The Bandrol, Pennant, or Flag, Fig. 8. The Sling, Fig. 9. The Thong, Fig. 10. and the Screw of the Bandrol, Fig. 11.

The Bandrol, attached to the Lance, was formerly an emblem, but is now the remains of chivalry: since the period of the introduction of Royal Banners into Europe, the birth, rank, or qualification of persons who were entitled to have Banners borne before them, varied their form. In the Crusades, the Knights Bannerets attached their heraldic armorial bearings, or those of the particular Order of Chivalry they belonged to, as Bandrols to their Lances, or emblazoned them thereon in a shield of pretence. (*Vide Appendix.*) In Poland, where the Lance is still the national arm, from the eleventh to the eighteenth century the nobility alone were permitted to serve in the Cavalry as Lancers; and they were authorized to attach their Banners, in the shape of an angular divided streamer, as Bandrols to their Lances.   The Standards appropriated to Regiments of Cavalry, at the present period, are truly emblematical of the very ancient and highly honorable equipments with the Lance, Officers being particularly selected to carry them, and their formation and mounting is exactly similar to the Lances borne by the Knights Bannerets in the age of Chivalry.

The following Rules and Regulations for the Exercise and Manœuvres of the Lance, are entirely compiled from the admirable Polish system of the late MARSHAL PRINCE JOSEPH PONIATOWSKI, and GENERAL COUNT CORVIN KRASINSKI; the latter now in the Service of the Emperor of Russia; they will be found as nearly adapted as possible to the present plan of Exercise with the Sabre; and the constant and uniform practice of both the Lance and the Sword Exercises will evidently prove the decided superiority of the Lance, combined with the Sabre, for the equipment of particular Regiments of Light Cavalry. That part which relates to Skirmishers, is the complete and correct British system, no innovation in, or deviation from it, being either material or necessary; to which has been added every regulation relative to manœuvring with, and wielding the Lance, as it comprises a considerable portion of the Drill Instructions.   In the British Service, where the men, the horses, and the appointments of the Cavalry are so decidedly superior to all those of other nations, there appeared nothing to be wanting but the introduction of the Lance,* and a trial of that arm, (which now forms a part of the Cavalry armament of all other European powers,) to render the British Tactique as complete as it is superior to that of every other nation, and, if it were possible, give perfection to the Drill and Exercise now practised and fixed by his Majesty for the Instruction of the Cavalry.   It is well known throughout the continent of Europe, that the fate of battles has been decided by the timely intervention of this newly revived, but very ancient arm; and that after victories have been obtained, the consequent results of harassing the enemy, and following up retreats, have been best performed by Regiments of Lancers.

---

* The four Regiments of British Lancers were formed in 1816, since the presentation of this Treatise, in manuscript, to His Royal Highness the Duke of York, in 1814.

In forming the following Treatise, I have endeavoured to arrange the Exercise and Manœuvres of the Lance throughout with the *greatest care, and most minute military precision;* and, at the same time, to make it correspond in every respect with the tactics of the British Service. Having had the most frequent opportunities, during my captivity in France, to witness the Reviews, Drills, and Exercise of the celebrated Polish Lancers, I have faithfully combined, in Six Divisions of Exercise, their very excellent and chevaleresque Manœuvres; and by implicitly adapting them to the Formations, Movements, and Exercise of the British Cavalry, I have added whatever, I trust, will be found truly essential and requisite to form expert Regiments of Lancers: in doing this, my only aim has been the happiness and gratification of serving His Majesty and my Country, by introducing the use of the Lance into the British Service, where, from the well-known excellence of both men and horses, the introduction of this effective and very warlike arm, combined with the present Instruction of the Sword, will, if it were possible, render the British Cavalry, now so highly esteemed, and the most superior, in every respect, in the world, more dreadful in the attack, and invincible when opposed to the Enemy.

———————

IN consequence of the very great imperfections of the Lance Exercise at present practised, (particularly the three Pimlico Divisions, so universally found fault with,) I have been requested by my military friends to publish the following Treatise, which I had the honor to present to His Royal Highness the Duke of York, in manuscript, at his Levee at the Horse Guards, on the 23rd of May, 1814, and which comprises the complete Polish Exercise and Manœuvres of the Lance.

The Six Divisions of Exercise are exactly the same as that active and expert Lancer, Serjeant Major Robert Cooke of the 9th Lancers, drilled a detachment of that Regiment in at Hampton Court, in 1816, according to the Polish system, under my superintendence, and in which he gave me the greatest satisfaction in every respect. As a distinguishing reward due to real military merit, and in justice to so truly deserving a Non-commissioned Officer, I thus openly and honorably bear testimony to his merits and talents in the strongest manner, as being a most valuable, intelligent, and excellent Soldier.

In submitting this Treatise to the Military world, it would afford me sincere pleasure
if I could thus publicly return thanks to the superior Officers of the Regiment I had
the honor to belong to, (The Earl of Rosslyn and Lieutenant Colonel Morland, 9th
Lancers,) for their attention to me at the period of my greatest exertions to introduce
the use and excellence of the Lance into His Majesty's Service. The *encouragement*
I received from them was very far different from what, I presume, I merited for my
efforts for the sole good of their, and my own, identical Regiment, and the British
Cavalry, which has since been fully proved, and which I now openly and ingenuously
submit to be fairly judged of by the Military in general. The remembrance of the
dignified contrast and generous support I experienced from the really Most Noble the
Marquis of Anglesey, Major General Sir Henry Torrens, and the Honorable Major
George de Blaquiere, will ever be preserved by me in an inverse ratio of recollection
from the adverse treatment I encountered, and which pleasing remembrance I can only
define in these very beautiful lines, truly expressive of the real gratitude I shall ever feel
for such highly honorable and distinguished support:

> " Antè leves ergo pascentur in æthere cervi,
> Et freta destituent nudos in littore pisces;
> Antè, pererratis amborum finibus, exul
> Aut Ararim Parthus bibet, aut Germania Tigrim,
> Quàm nostro *illorum* labatur pectore vultus.
>
> Virg. Ecl. 1. Ver. 60, &c.

R. H. de M.

CONTENTS.

PART I.

PART II.

PART III.

PART IV.

PART V.

PART VI.

PART VII.

PART VIII.

PART IX.

APPENDIX.

DIRECTIONS FOR PLACING THE PLATES.

THE whole of the Plates, the Frontispiece and Illustrative Design excepted, to be either bound up together at the end of the Work, or arranged as follow:

FRONTISPIECE,
PRINCE JOSEPH PONIATOWSKI,
To face the Title.

DESIGN ILLUSTRATIVE OF THE WORK,
" Palmam qui meruit, ferat."
To face the back of the Title.

DIMENSIONS OF THE LANCE.

PLATE I.

		Feet.	Inches.
Fig. 1.	LENGTH of the Spear,		9
	Breadth at the base,		$1\frac{1}{4}$
2.	Length of the Socket of the Spear,		$3\frac{1}{2}$
	Breadth at the neck,		$0\frac{3}{4}$
	Diameter of the base,		$1\frac{1}{8}$
3.	Circumference of the Ball of the Spear,		6
	Diameter of Ditto,		$1\frac{7}{8}$
4.	Length of the great Bandlet,	2	
	Breadth,		$0\frac{1}{2}$
5.	Length of the counter Bandlet,	1	6
	Breadth,		$0\frac{1}{2}$
6.	Length of the Shaft, (before mounting,)	8	$3\frac{1}{2}$
	Ditto, (when mounted,)	7	5
	Diameter,		$1\frac{1}{4}$
7.	Length of the Socket of the Butt, or Ferrule,		7
	Diameter, at the top,		1
8.	Depth of the Bandrol,	1	1
	Breadth,	2	$7\frac{1}{2}$
	Length of the sides of the angular cut,	1	$5\frac{1}{2}$
9.	Full length of the Sling,	2	8
	Length for Exercise and Service when doubled,*	1	2
	Overplus for laying on the Shaft,		4
	Breadth,		$0\frac{3}{4}$
10.	The Thong, (no specific length,)		
	Length in general of the Lance,	9	

The Screw of the Bandrol, Plate 1, Fig. 11, is drawn corresponding to its proper size.

* No unnecessary length should be allowed, being very dangerous in the ranks when the Sling is too long; and the Sling should be placed on the Shaft, exactly on a line with the Lancer's shoulder when on foot.

PARTICULAR EXPLANATION OF PLATE 19.

Fig. 1. THE Oriflamme of St. Dennis.

    2. The Banner of the Knights of Malta.

    3. The Banner of the Knights Templars.

    4. The Banner of the Teutonic Knights.

    5. The Banner of Ancient Montmorency, as likewise that of the Knights Bannerets, with the difference, that each Knight bore his own proper Heraldic Armorial Bearings, as a Bandrol attached to his Lance. *Vide Appendix.*

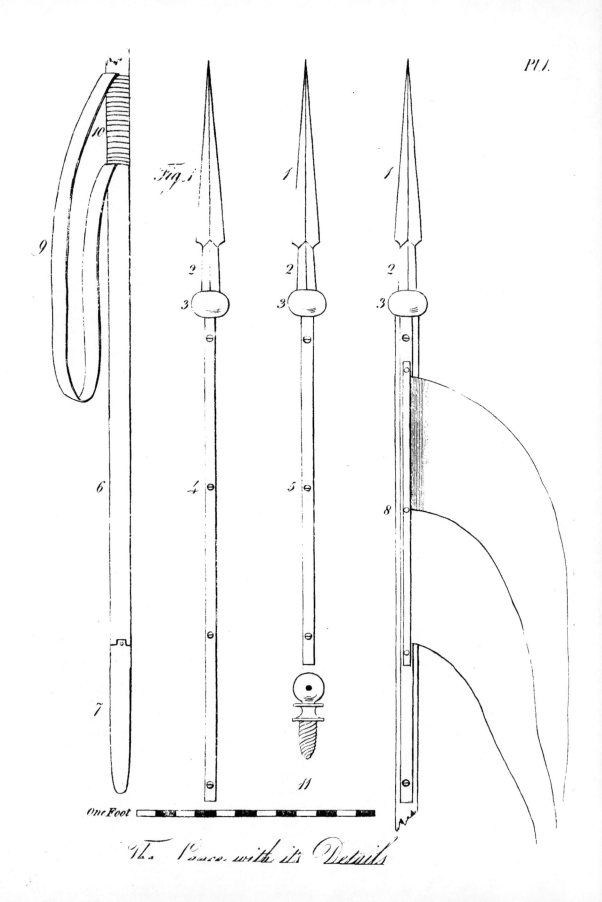

Pl. I.

Fig. 1

One Foot

The Lance with its Details

RULES AND REGULATIONS

FOR THE

EXERCISE AND MANŒUVRES

OF THE

LANCE.

PART I.

Formation of Regiments.

THE assembling of Troops, Squadrons, and Regiments of Lancers, will be entirely conformable to His Majesty's Instructions and Regulations for the Formations and Movements of the Cavalry.

The principles of the Drill and of the Sword Exercise will likewise be the same in every respect.

B

Position of the Lancer on Foot.

THE position of the Lancer on foot, on receiving the word " *Attention*," will be erect, preserving the equal squareness of the shoulders and the body to the front ; the heels on a line, and closed ; the knees straight, without stiffness ; the toes a little turned out ; the feet forming an angle of 60 degrees ; the arms hanging near the body, but not stiff; the flat part of the hand and the little finger touching the thigh ; the thumbs as far back as the seams of the breeches ; the elbows and the shoulders kept back ; the belly drawn in ; the breast advanced, but without constraint ; the body upright, inclining forward, so that the weight of it principally bears on the forepart of the feet ; the head well up, and neither turned to the right or left.

The Lance will be placed in the position " *Rest Lances*," supported by the right hand falling naturally ; the shaft fixed perpendicularly in the hollow of the right shoulder ; the butt rested upon the ground, and about one inch from the point of the right foot ; the left hand hanging by the side, over the sword, which may be raised up, and hung upon the hook of the sword-belt.

Lance Exercise on Foot.

<table>
<tr><td>WORDS OF COMMAND.</td><td>MOTIONS.</td><td></td></tr>
<tr><td>Carry Lances.</td><td>1.</td><td>SEIZE the Lance with the right hand; the hand on a line with the shoulder; the elbow and fore-arm well closed upon the shaft, and the Lance held perfectly perpendicular.</td></tr>
<tr><td>Rest Lances.</td><td>1.</td><td>Bring back the right hand to its original position.</td></tr>
<tr><td>Advance Lances.</td><td>1.</td><td>Place the right hand, as quick as possible, behind the shaft, and the fore-finger in front.</td></tr>
<tr><td></td><td>2.</td><td>Raise the Lance with the right hand in one motion, and with as little appearance of effort as possible, about two inches from the ground; the right hand holding it with a firm grasp about two feet from the butt; the arm lightly extended; the wrist turned downwards; the thumb in front upon the shaft; the fore-finger extended upon the side; the others underneath, and the shaft fixed perpendicularly in the hollow of the right shoulder.</td></tr>
</table>

Present Lances.   1.   Bring the Lance with the right hand opposite the left eye; seize it briskly with the left, the right hand close under the left elbow; the thumb and fore-finger extended upon the shaft, and the Lance held perfectly perpendicular.

2.   Let the Lance fall diagonally across the body; the fore and middle fingers of the right hand extended in front along the shaft; the left hand resting on the left breast; the thumb extended upon the shaft; the butt raised about four inches from the ground; draw back the right foot at the same instant, so that the hollow of it may touch the left heel.

Advance Lances.   1.   Bring back the Lance with both hands into the hollow of the right shoulder; replace the right hand, and bring up the right foot at the same instant to its original position.

2.   Quit the Lance with the left hand, which will fall briskly in its place.

WORDS OF COMMAND.	MOTIONS.	
* *Guard.*	1.	Make a half face to the right.
	2.	Throw the Lance with the right hand into the left, which will seize it about eighteen inches from the right; the left elbow close to the side; the upper part of the body rather inclined forward; the right wrist rested against the hip; the Lance held in nearly a horizontal position; the point rather elevated, and on a line with the right eye.

At the second motion, the rear rank will bring the right heel six inches on that side, and about three inches behind the left; they will drop their Lances, so that they will fall between their front rank files and the files on their right, without touching either.

Advance Lances.	1.	Turn upon the left heel to regain the proper front, bringing up the right foot at

* " *Charge Lances*" is, in my opinion, more appropriate and preferable, in the British service, as corresponding with " *Charge Bayonets.*"—The chivalric terms are " *Couch Lances,*" " *Charge Lances,*" and " *Cross Lances ;*" the latter term is adopted by the French, their words of command being " *Croisez Lances,*" " *Croisez Bayonettes ;*" and the Polish word implies, in English, " *Charge Lances,*" which certainly has a more military sound and signification than " *Guard.*"

WORDS OF COMMAND.	MOTIONS.	
		the same instant to its original position ; replace the Lance with the left hand in the hollow of the right shoulder, and re-seize it with the right hand, as already laid down.
	2.	Quit the Lance with the left hand, which will fall briskly in its place.
Rest Lances.	1.	Let the Lance fall to the ground in the right hand, which will support it naturally in its original position.
Carry Lances.		As already laid down.
Trail Lances.	1.	Raise the Lance about two inches from the ground ; lower it rather forwards, so that it will take a diagonal direction ; the spear upwards, inclined to the front, and the butt downwards to the rear.
		The Lance may be brought to this position for ordinary purposes ; such as marching or taking short distances, and when manœuvring at double quick time.

WORDS OF COMMAND.	MOTIONS.

Rest Lances.   1.   Let the Lance fall to the ground, throwing it into its original position with the right hand.

* *Shoulder Lances.* 1.   Quit the position of the right hand, which will re-seize the Lance about two feet from the butt; the hand reversed; the thumb above upon the shaft; the fingers underneath; the Lance held in a diagonal position; the shaft rested upon the right shoulder; the butt raised about six inches from the ground, inclined rather forward, and the spear to the rear.

Rest Lances.   1.   Let the Lance fall to the ground, bringing it, at the same time, to its original position with the right hand.

The positions " *Rest*," " *Carry*," " *Trail*," and " *Shoulder Lances*," will be practised likewise with the left hand on that side, the Lancers being frequently obliged to have recourse to them for ordinary purposes.

---

* The Polish word of command is " *Slope Lances*," which is more appropriate and preferable, as " *Shoulder Lances*" signifies bringing the Lance to a perpendicular position against the right shoulder, as in " *Shoulder Arms*," whereas " *Slope Lances*" implies the proper vertical sloped position.

When the Lancers receive the order to " *Stand at Ease*," they will assume the usual position, letting the Lance rest upon the right shoulder when in the position " *Rest Lances*," and bringing it with the right hand across the body in front, when in that of " *Advance Lances*."

At the word " *Attention*," they will resume the original position they changed from, when they will be exercised in the different manœuvres of the Lance, which will be practised and executed successively on foot, in the same manner as laid down under the heads of " LANCE EXERCISE ON HORSEBACK," and " DIVISIONS OF EXERCISE."

When a Regiment, Squadron, or Division is assembled for exercise, the officers and non-commissioned officers charged with the drill, will successively disengage their Divisions, and march them to their respective exercising grounds, which must be taken up in such a manner, that they will not interfere with each other.

When the Divisions have arrived, and are halted and dressed, they will proceed to perform the Lance Exercise, by word of command ; observing always, as a general rule, that the Lances are brought to the position " *Trail Lances*," previous to commencing the manœuvres of the Lance, and that the motions are taken, throughout, from Fleugelmen, according to the principles of the Sword Exercise.

The head must follow the direction of every motion ; should the line be extensive, two Fleugelmen will be necessary, one on each flank, who are to be careful to take up the time from each other, according to the different changes of position, or dressing points from right to left.

The distance of ranks and files will then be taken, as laid down for the Exercise and Manœuvres of the Lance in Battalion, Squadron, and smaller Divisions.

The Battalion, Squadron, or Division, will be told off by wings, ranks of threes, and right and left files.

Distance of Ranks and Files on Foot.

WORDS OF COMMAND.

Rear Rank,
Take Distance for
Lance Exercise.

THE right and left flank Lancers of the rear rank, belonging to both wings, will face about, and retreat fourteen paces,* dressing by the right.

---

* The rear rank, when at close order, should always be one pace of 30 inches distant from the front rank, which will complete the actual distance between the front and rear ranks to fifteen paces,

WORDS OF COMMAND.

March.

·The rear rank will be faced to the right about, then take their distance at ordinary, quick, or double quick time; halt, front,* and dress by the pivots: the Fleugelmen, at the same time, will advance to the front.

From the Centre of Battalion, Squadron, or Division, Open your Files. March.

The Lancers will receive the order to come to the position, " *Carry Lances,*" and afterwards to that of " *Trail Lances,*" previous to receiving the word " *March,*" after which both wings will open out, gradually extending their right arms to the full extent; the Lance firmly grasped in the right hand, held perfectly perpendicular when extended, and rested upon the ground, the whole will open out in such a manner, that each man's Lance will be about six inches distant from the point of the left shoulder of the file on his right, and his hand on a line with it.

---

* A considerable improvement is suggested, of drilling the Lancers to front " *to the Left About,*" as the centre and left threes incline so much to the left on their march to the rear, that on arriving at their prescribed distance, they are almost faced to the left, or half faced to the left about. This would prevent any irregularity in those ranks in completing the conversion, some of whom always front to the " *Right,*" and others to the " *Left About.*"

The rear rank will do the same, taking care to cover their front rank files correctly.

The arms will be kept extended till the drill officer sees that the distances are perfectly correct, when they will be withdrawn to the position, " *Carry Lances*," by a motion from the right Fleugelman. The drill officer previously giving the word, " *Eyes Right*."

The greatest attention possible is requisite to insure the proper distance of files, in order that no serious or unpleasant accident may occur on proving the distance, preparatory to taking which, the Lancers will receive the order to come from the position, " *Carry*" to that of "*Trail Lances*."

Prepare to perform Lance Exercise.

At this word of command, the right subdivision of each wing, and the left subdivision of the line, will mark the distance of files in the following manner :

The right flank file of ranks by threes

c 2

will stand fast; the centre file will face to the right about, take five paces to the rear of the right flank file, front, and cover him.

The left file of ranks by threes will likewise face to the right about, retreat ten paces, front, and cover the two preceding files of the sub-division; the left sub-division of the Battalion or Squadron will do the same.

The rear rank will do the same, taking care to cover their front rank files correctly.

March.

The whole of the right files of ranks by threes, belonging to both ranks, will stand fast; the centre and left files, only, taking their distances as before directed, taking care to cover correctly, and dress by the pivots.

The officers and non-commissioned officers will retire to the rear, except otherwise ordered by the commanding officer.

The non-commissioned officers will be three paces to the rear, covering a file, and equally distributed behind their respective troops or squadrons.

The officers will be at the distance of six paces, distributed in like manner in the rear of, and between the intervals of, the non-commissioned officers.

The trumpeters will remain in their usual places on the right of the Battalion, Squadron, or Division.

The Battalion, Squadron, or Division, thus arranged, will be formed in an open column, six deep.

The Lancers will then receive the order to come to the Position, " *Guard*," preparatory to proving the distance of ranks and files.

To the Right, prove Distance of Files.

The whole of the Lancers of the Battalion, Squadron, or Division, belonging to both ranks, (the right flank files excepted, who, having no distance to prove, will remain in the Position, " *Guard*," *)* taking the motions from the right Fleugelman, will give point to the right, with the full extent of the arm, preserving the nearly horizontal position of the Lance, the point rather elevated, the bandrol or flag downwards, and the shaft held in the precise manner as when giving point in that direction ; the body and the eyes to be turned gently to the right.

When each file has had time to see whether he has his proper distance, and corrected it where required, the Lancers will receive the order to return to the Position, " *Guard.*"

Guard.

At the word of command, " *Guard*," the Lances will be withdrawn together to the position directed, taking the time from the right Fleugelman ; in doing which the point and bandrol are not to be dropped ; the body to be returned square to the front.

To the Front,
Prove Distance of Files.

The distance will then be proved to the front, by giving point in that direction, according to the rules laid down under the head of " *Front give Point,*" pushing the Lance forward with caution, so as not to wound the file in front, should the distance not have been preserved ; the body gently inclined forwards ; the front rank will remain in the Position, " *Guard,*" having no distance to prove.

Guard.

The Lances will be retired to the Position, " *Guard,*" without dropping the point and bandrol ; the body to be returned square to the front.

It must be observed, as a general rule, in the course of the different motions of the Lance Exercise on foot, that the bridle-hand of the Lancer is held precisely in the same position as when holding the reins of his horse, crossing the body in that direction ; the nails inwards, the hand closed, and the heels six inches asunder.

After the Lance Exercise on foot is performed, the Battalion, Squadron, or Division, will receive orders to come to the Position,

" *Trail Lances*," and will resume its proper formation in ordinary, quick, or double quick time, in the following manner:

Front form Line,
or Squadron.
March.

The right files of ranks by threes, belonging to both ranks, will stand fast; the centre and left files will advance from column, form line, and dress by the pivots.

Rear Rank, close Order.
March.

The rear rank will close to the front, to within one pace, in the usual manner.

To the Right (Left or
Centre) of Battalion,
Squadron, or Division,
close your Files.
March.

The files will close, if in Squadron or Division, by the side step, to the right, left, or inwards, or by facing the Lancers in the necessary direction, and to march, halt, front, and align them.

Should the Battalion have taken distance from the centre " *Outwards*," in order to open its files, the order will be given to close them to the centre " *Inwards*," by the side step, or by facing the Lancers in the necessary direction, and forming.

When the ranks are at close order, the

WORDS OF COMMAND.

Lancers will be dressed by the right, should their formation be either in Line or Division; but if in Squadron, they may be more correctly dressed by the centre, after which they will receive the word " *Eyes Front.*"

The Battalion, Squadron, or Division, being aligned and dressed, may then receive the order to come to the Position, " *Rest Lances,*" and " *Stand at Ease.*"

Should the Divisions not be sufficiently strong, so as to require being manœuvred by ranks of threes, or for private drill, where the space is not confined, the Lancers will receive orders to come from the Position, " *Carry,*" to that of " *Trail Lances,*" and may take distance in the manner laid down under the following head.

Polish Method of Taking Distance.

WORDS OF COMMAND.

Rear Rank,
take Distance for
Lance Exercise.

THE right and left flank Lancers of the rear rank, belonging to both wings, will face outwards about, and retreat four paces, dressing by the right.

D

WORDS OF COMMAND.

March.

The rear rank will be faced to the " *Right About ;*" then take their distance at ordinary, quick, or double quick time, as may be ordered previous to the word " *March ;*" and will afterwards receive the order to halt, front, and dress by the pivots ; the Fleugelmen at the same time will advance to the front.

From the Right, (Left, or Centre,) of Divisions, extend your Files.

If " *From the Right,*" the whole of the Lancers belonging to both ranks, the right flank files excepted, will be faced to the left ;* if " *From the Left,*" *vice versâ ;* and if " *From the Centre,*" outwards, first fixing upon a centre point, which, if a man, he will remain perfectly steady.

March.

At the word " *March,*" the Lancers will advance, and be followed successively by all those of their respective ranks, (the right flank files excepted, who being on the

---

* Or, at the word, " *From the Right extend your Files,*" the whole of the Lancers, the right flank files excepted, will advance the right heel into the hollow of the left foot, preparatory to facing to the left, then look to the right Fleugelman for the signal to face, without waiting for any other word of command.

opposite wing from that to which the movement is made, and having no distance to take, will remain perfectly steady,) and, in advancing, they will cast a glance of the eye from their right to their rear, so as to take up an interval of five paces, and will regulate the distance for their formation upon the Lancer who is immediately in their rear: the second Lancers from the standing flanks, having marched five paces, will halt and front of their own accord, except otherwise ordered, and align themselves upon the right flank files of their respective ranks, who, by remaining steady, will serve as pivots to dress by: the third Lancers, by casting a glance of the eye from their right to their rear, will likewise halt and front five paces from the second, and align themselves upon those already formed; the remainder of the Lancers, belonging to both ranks, will successively do the like, dressing themselves upon the three first.

The Lancers may likewise extend their files by the side step, from the right, left, or centre, " *Outwards,*" each Lancer halting of his own accord, when he has judged and taken his distance of five paces, and dressing by the point he forms upon, after which the Divisions will receive the word, " *By the Right Dress,*" and then, " *Eyes Front.*"

The Lancers will then receive the order to come to the Position, " *Guard,*" after which the distance of ranks and files will be proved, as already laid down.

After the Lance Exercise on Foot is performed, the Divisions, when they are not told off and manœuvred by ranks of threes, will receive orders to come to the position, " *Trail Lances,*" and will resume their proper formation in the following manner :

POLISH METHOD.

Rear Rank, close Order. March.

THE rear rank will close to the front, to within one pace, in the usual manner.

To the Right, (Left, or Centre,) Close your Files.

If " *To the Right,*" the whole of the Lancers belonging to both ranks, the right flank files excepted, will be faced to the right; if " *To the Left*," *vice versa*; and if " *To the Centre*" inwards, first fixing upon a centre point, as already laid down, in order to resume their original formation.

March.

At the word " *March*," they will close their files, halt and front of their own accord, except otherwise ordered, and align themselves, dressing by the point they receive orders to form upon, after which they will receive the word, " *Eyes Front.*"

The Divisions being aligned and dressed, may then receive the order to come to the position, " *Rest Lances*," and " *Stand at Ease.*"

MOUNTING

AND

TELLING OFF IN SQUADRON.

PART II.

Position of the Lancer previous to Mounting.

Stand to your Horses.

THIS being the first position previous to mounting, each Lancer will place himself on the near side of his horse, in a line with his shoulders; the reins passed over his neck; the whip on the near side; the right hand holding the bridon rein, about two inches from the bitt; the back of the hand uppermost, taking up, in every other respect, the usual position when " *Standing at Ease;*" the Lance rested upon the left shoulder, and the sword hanging at the full length of the slings, in its natural position.

WORDS OF COMMAND.

Attention.

At the word " *Attention*," the Lancers will instantly take up the proper unconstrained position of the soldier, placing themselves perfectly square to the front, and coming to the position, " *Rest Lances*" with the left hand, the right holding the bridon rein in the position when " *Standing to Horse ;*" the whole will then remain perfectly steady and attentive, dressing by the right; after which they will receive the word " *Eyes Front.*"

Carry Lances.

Pl. 2.

Seize the Lance with the left hand ; the hand on a line with the shoulder ; the elbow and fore-arm well closed upon the shaft ; the Lance held perfectly perpendicular ; the butt rested upon the ground, and about one inch from the point of the left foot.

Tell off by Files.

The Lancers will then receive orders to " *Tell off by Files*," preparatory to taking their mounting distance.

Pl. 2.

Position of the Lancer Previous to Mounting.

Mounting.

WORDS OF COMMAND.

Prepare to Mount.

THE left files will rein back according to order; the whole of the Lancers then coming to the position, " *Trail Lances*" with the left hand, face to the right, and without letting go the Lance, seize the bitt rein with the left hand, and quit it with the right; re-seize the bitt rein then with the right hand, to equalize the length of the sides; place it in the left hand, just under the right, the little finger between the reins, and the back of the hand towards the horse's head; lower the left hand, and draw the bitt rein through it with the right to feel the horse's mouth; throw the whip gently over the pommel of the saddle to the off side, and raise the butt of the Lance about ten inches from the ground; seize a lock of the horse's mane with the right hand, put it into the left, twist it round the thumb, and shift the Lance at the same time with the right hand through the left,

E

WORDS OF COMMAND.

to grasp it firm with it exactly in its centre of gravity; take hold of the stirrup leather, just above the iron, with the right hand; place one-third of the left foot in the stirrup, resting the knee against the horse's shoulder; support the weight of the body upon the toe of the right foot, and place the right hand upon the cantle of the saddle.

Mount.

Rise upon the right foot, pulling the horse's mane, at the same time, forcibly towards the body, and rest the right hand firmly upon the cantle of the saddle to prevent it from turning; bring the body upright, and look well over the horse; pass the right leg, well extended, over the horse's croup without touching it, and move gently into the seat, changing the hand, at the same time, from the cantle of the saddle to the off holster; the thumb within and the fingers without; place the right foot gently in the stirrup without stooping to do it with the right hand; quit the horse's mane with the left hand, and make sure of the bitt rein with

Pl.3.

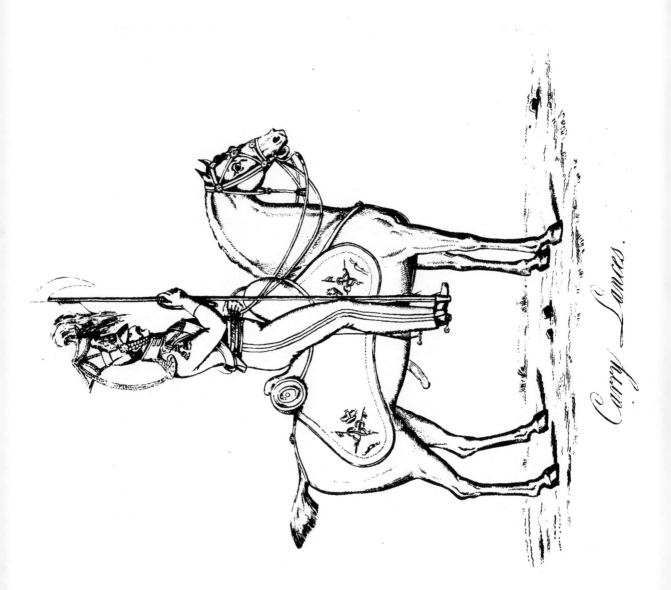

Carry Lances — him.

WORDS OF COMMAND.　MOTIONS.　it, without letting go the Lance; press the reins between the thumb and the joint of the fore-finger, and raise the bridle-hand so as to feel the horse's mouth.

Carry Lances.　1.　Seize the Lance quickly with the right hand, at the full extent of the arm, low down under the left, between the reins and the horse's neck, letting it go with the bridle-hand; the body upright.

2.　Raise the Lance perpendicularly with a brisk motion of the right hand; pass it about four inches over the horse's neck, close to the front of the saddle; place the butt in the boot or bucket attached to the off

Pl. 3.　stirrup, and raise the right hand on a line with the shoulder; the elbow about eight inches from the shaft; the thumb in the sling; the fingers closed, and the Lance held perfectly perpendicular; the head well up; the body well back, preserving its natural pliability and proper balance, and take up, instantly, the position of the Lancer on horseback.

WORDS OF COMMAND. MOTIONS.

Left Files, Front Form.
March.

At the word, " *March*," the left files will advance into their ranks without hurry or confusion, the right files, at the same time, will raise their bridle-hands to feel their horses' mouths, and close their legs to them to prevent them from moving.

(Right Arm,)
Sling Lances.

Pl. 4.

1. Pass the right arm through the sling, and cast the Lance to the rear with a brisk motion of the arm, so that it will hang about midway between the elbow and the shoulder, the right hand resting upon the thick part of the thigh; the thumb to the rear, and the fingers in front.

Sit at Ease.

According to order, or the Lancers may come to the position, " *Rest Lances*," on the right side, in order to " *Sit at Ease*," as follows, without waiting for that word of command.

Rest Lances.

1. Let the Lance fall into the hollow of the right shoulder, the right hand dropping down to the full extent upon the shaft; the thumb and fingers extended down-

Pl. 4

Slimg — Lances.

29

WORDS OF COMMAND. MOTIONS. wards, and the back of the hand to the front.

The Lancers will likewise be practised in mounting at the off side, which will correspond precisely with the rules laid down for the near side, with the difference, that the left leg, in mounting, is to be thrown well extended over the horse's croup, and the left hand is to assist, at the same time, in passing the sword over the croup, to the near side, in the rear of the Lancer. The trifling motions to be reversed will naturally and instinctively point themselves out to the Lancers.

After the word, " *Sit at Ease*" is given, the Lancers will receive orders to " *Take up their Reins*," and see that every thing is in order, previous to their being told off in Squadron, and taking their distance of ranks and files, after which they will then receive the preparatory words of command.

Attention.
Carry Lances.
By the Right,
(Centre, or Left,)
Dress.
Eyes front.

After having assumed the position, "*Carry Lances,*" from that of "*Sling Lances,*" as hereafter laid down, when the word "*By the Right, (Centre, or Left,) Dress,*" is given, the Lancers will, of their own accord, change to the position "*Rest Lances,*" in order to dress correctly, and at the word "*Eyes Front,*" they will again resume that of "*Carry Lances,*" without waiting for that word of command.

The Regiment or Squadron will then receive the order to "*Tell off in Squadron,*" according to the rules of the Service. Should a Troop or Division, only, be present, they may be told off in a minor degree, but if either are sufficiently strong, they should always, in such case, be told off by ranks of threes, and right and left files, previous to taking their distance of ranks and files.

The motions throughout the Lance Exercise on Horseback, will be executed slowly at first, the drill officers taking particular care to explain them to the Lancers with a loud voice, and in an intelligible manner, and never permitting them to change from one manœuvre to another, previous to their having fully comprehended the preceding ones.

When a Regiment is perfectly drilled, the Lance Exercise on Horseback may be performed by the sound of the trumpet or bugle; at field days or private drills, the Regiment may be broke into Divisions, when officers and steady non-commissioned officers will be appointed to drill them, always taking care that the exercising ground is divided in such a manner, that the Divisions will not interfere with each other.

Before the Lance Exercise is attempted to be performed on horseback, it will be necessary to render the horses steady by accustoming them to the sight of the bandrol or flag, which is easily effected by frequently dropping the Lance before their eyes, both on the near and the off side; they must never be checked or spurred on account of their being frightened at the appearance of it at first, but by degrees brought to bear the sight of it, and made much of, caressed, and encouraged in proportion as they become steady and tractable, which measure will be easily effected, in a very short period, by gentle means alone.

The distance of ranks and files, on horseback, will then be taken in the manner laid down under the following head.

Distance of Ranks and Files on Horseback.

Rear Rank,
take Distance for
Lance Exercise.

THE right and left flank Lancers of the rear rank, belonging to both wings, will turn their horses outwards about, take five horses' lengths to the rear, front inwards about, and dress by the right.

March.

The rear rank will rein back and dress by the pivots; the Fleugelmen, at the same time, will advance to the front.

From the Centre of the
Regiment, Squadron,
or Division,
open your Files.
March.

The whole of the Lancers belonging to both wings will instantly open out, by passaging their horses outwards to the distance of nine inches from knee to knee.

The rear rank will do the same, taking care to cover their front rank files correctly.

Prepare to perform
Lance Exercise.

The right and left sub-division of each wing will mark the distance of files as directed for the Lance Exercise on Foot, allowing an interval of one horse's length between head and croup.

The rear rank will do the same, taking care to cover their front rank files correctly.

March.

The whole of the right files of ranks by threes, belonging to both ranks, will stand fast; the centre and left files will rein back till clear of the standing flanks, they will then pass to the right, form on, and dress by the pivots, taking care to cover correctly, by placing their horses square to the front.

The officers and the standard will advance to the front, as at open order, and will be divided in a line at equal distances, one horse's length in front of their respective Squadrons.

The officer commanding the Squadron will be advanced one horse's length in front of the standard.

The non-commissioned officers will re-

F

main in their usual places in Squadron, or they may be replaced by privates from the flanks.

The serjeant-majors and the serrefiles will be divided in a line at equal distances, one horse's length from the rear rank; the former on the outward flanks of their respective Squadrons.

The farriers will be one horse's length in the rear of the serrefiles.

The trumpeters will remain in their usual places, on the right of the Regiment, Squadron, or Division.

The Regiment, Squadron, or Division, thus arranged, will be formed in an open column, six deep.

The Lancers will then receive the order to come to the Position, " *Carry Lances*," from that of " *Sling Lances*,"* if not pre-

---

* When the word, " *Sling Lances*," alone, is given, it will always imply on the *right arm*.

WORDS OF COMMAND. MOTIONS.

viously assumed, and afterwards to the Position, "*Guard,*" preparatory to proving the distance of files.

Carry Lances. 1.

Drive the Lance forward with a brisk motion of the right arm; seize it backhanded, with the right hand reversed to the front, and the thumb downwards; disengage the right arm from the sling, and re-seize the Lance briskly, with a firm grasp, with the right hand; place the butt in the boot or bucket attached to the off stirrup, and raise the right hand on a line with the shoulder; the elbow about eight inches from the shaft; the thumb in the sling; the fingers closed, and the Lance held perfectly perpendicular.

Guard.

As laid down under the head of " LANCE EXERCISE ON HORSEBACK."

The distance of ranks and files will then be proved " *To the Right,*" and " *To the Front,*" in the same manner as laid down for the " LANCE EXERCISE ON FOOT."

F 2

WORDS OF COMMAND. MOTIONS.

Guard.

The Lances will be withdrawn to the Position, " *Guard*," after proving the distance of ranks and files, without dropping the point and bandrol ; the body to be returned square to the front.

After the Lance Exercise on Horseback is performed, the Regiment, Squadron, or Division, will receive orders to come to the Position, " *Carry*," or to that of " *Sling Lances*," and will resume its proper formation, at either a walk, trot, or gallop, in the following manner :

WORDS OF COMMAND.

Front form Line,
or Squadron.
March.

The right files of ranks by threes, belonging to both ranks, will stand fast ; the centre and left files will advance from column, form line, and dress by the pivots.

Rear Rank, close Order.
March.

The rear rank will close to the front, to within half a horse's length, in the usual manner.

To the Right, (Left, or
Centre,) of the Regiment,
Squadron, or Division,
close your Files.
March.

The files will close, if in Squadron or Division, by passaging their horses to the right, left, or inwards, or by filing in the necessary direction, and forming.

Should the Regiment have taken distance from the centre, " *Outwards*," in order to open its files, the order will be given to close them to the centre, " *Inwards*," by passaging, or by filing, and forming.

When the ranks are at close order, the Lancers will be dressed by the right, should their formation be either in Line or Division; but if in Squadron, they may be more correctly dressed by the centre, after which they will receive the word, " *Eyes Front.*"

The Regiment, Squadron, or Division, being aligned and dressed, if the commanding officer's intention is not to dismount them, may then receive the order, if not previously given, to come to the Position, " *Sling*," or to that of " *Rest Lances*," and " *Sit at Ease.*"

Should the Divisions not be sufficiently strong, so as to require being manœuvred by ranks of threes, or for private drill, where the space is not confined, the Lancers may take distance in the manner laid down under the following head.

Polish Method of Taking Distance.

WORDS OF COMMAND.

Rear Rank,
rein back,
(or take Distance,) for
Lance Exercise.

THE right and left flank Lancers of the rear rank, belonging to both wings, will rein back one horse's length, dressing by the right.

March.

The rear rank will rein back, and dress by the pivots ; the Fleugelmen at the same time will advance to the front.

From the Right,
(Left, or Centre,)
of Divisions,
extend your Files.

If " *From the Right,*" the whole of the Lancers belonging to both ranks, the right flank files excepted, will incline their horses to the left, at the word, " *Left File ;*" if " *From the Left,*" vice versa ; and if " *From the Centre,*" outwards, first fixing upon a centre point, which, if a man, he will remain perfectly steady.

March.

At the word " *March,*" the Lancers will advance, and be followed successively by all those of their respective ranks, (the right flank files excepted, who being on the opposite wing from that to which the movement is made, and having no distance to take, will remain perfectly steady,) and, in advancing, they will cast a glance of the eye from their right to their rear, so as to take up an interval of one horse's length, and will regulate the distance for their formation upon the Lancer who is immediately in their rear: the second Lancers from the standing flanks, having judged and taken their distance of one horse's length, will form to the right, and align themselves upon the right flank files of their respective ranks, who, by remaining steady, will serve as pivots to dress by : the third Lancers, by casting a glance of the eye from their right to their rear, and having judged their distance, will likewise form to the right, at one horse's length from the second, and align themselves upon those already formed ; the remainder of the Lancers, belonging to both ranks, will successively do the like, dressing themselves upon the three first.

The Lancers may likewise extend their files, by passaging their horses to the left, right, or from the centre, " *Outwards,*" each Lancer, halting of his own accord, when he has judged and taken his distance of one horse's length, and dressing by the point he forms upon, after which the Divisions will receive the word, " *By the Right Dress,*" and then, " *Eyes Front.*"

The Lancers will then receive the order, if not previously given, to come to the Position, " *Carry Lances,*" and then to that of " *Guard,*" after which the distance of ranks and files will be proved, as already laid down.

After the Lance Exercise on Horseback is performed, the Divisions, when they are not told off and manœuvred by ranks of threes, will receive orders to come to the Position, " *Carry,*" or to that of " *Sling Lances,*" and will resume their proper formation in the following manner :

POLISH METHOD.

Rear Rank, close Order.
March.

THE rear rank will close to the front, to within half a horse's length, in the usual manner.

To the Right,
(Left, or Centre,)
close your Files.

If " *To the Right*," the whole of the Lancers belonging to both ranks, the right flank files excepted, will incline their horses to the right, at the word, " *Right File ;*" if " *To the Left*," *vice versâ ;* and if " *To the Centre*," inwards, first fixing upon a centre point, as already laid down, in order to resume their original formation.

March.

At the word, " *March*," they will close their files, form up, and align themselves, dressing by the point they receive orders to form upon, after which they will receive the word, " *Eyes Front.*"

The Divisions being aligned and dressed, if the commanding officer's intention is not to dismount them, may then receive the order, if not previously given, to come to the Position, " *Sling*," or to that of " *Rest Lances*," and " *Sit at Ease.*"

G

LANCE EXERCISE

ON

HORSEBACK.

PART III.

Preliminary Instructions.

THE Regiment, Squadron, or Division, after performing each Manœuvre of the Lance Exercise on Horseback, will return to the Position, " *Guard;*" they will then remain perfectly steady and attentive.

The commanding officer, after a short pause, will repeat the next word of command, and so on, in like manner, throughout the whole Lance Exercise.

The reins must be held very short, so as to enable the Lancer, by the least action of the bridle-hand, to regulate the motions of his horse's head, in order to prevent the Lance from being obstructed in its course, and that the tightness of the reins may not occasion any reining back, or impatience in the animal, taking care to ease him, by carrying the hand sufficiently forward for that purpose, and at the same time feeling his mouth, without bearing a dead weight in that direction.

The Lance Exercise on Horseback must be performed slow at first, till great correctness of execution, and perfection in every motion, is attained.

In giving point, or parrying to the right or left of the front, the bridle-hand of the Lancer is to feel the horse's mouth in the opposite direction, in order to prevent the possibility of danger to the animal; if this is not done with judgment, the horse will become unsteady; the slightest inclination of the hand is sufficient for the purpose required, if the reins are properly held; there is no danger whatever of wounding the horse, provided the point of the Lance is directed outwards, and that the horse's mouth is felt in the opposite direction; or of its being impeded in moving it either to the front or rear, if attention is paid to give point to the front, clear of the horse's head, and taking care that the butt does not come in contact with it when giving point to the rear; it must likewise be observed, as a general rule, that the eyes follow the point in whatever direction it is given; too much attention cannot be paid to these particulars, as in their observance the safety of the animal and dexterity in the Exercise of the Lance, in a very great measure, depend; the Positions of all the manœuvres are precisely the same on horseback as they are on foot, that of " *Rest Lances*" excepted, which is very slightly varied to correspond with the position required, when " *Standing*" and " *Sitting at Ease.*"

The Lancers will likewise be drilled to come to the Position, " *Rest,*" " *Carry,*" and " *Shoulder Lances,*" with the left hand on the near side, they being essentially necessary, on several occasions, as well on horseback as on foot; for this purpose, with respect to the two first instances, there will be in all Regiments of Lancers a boot or bucket attached to the near, as well as to the off stirrup.

The Lance Exercise on Horseback may also be performed at a gallop, and in speed.

In giving point to the left, the horse is to be wheeled to the left about; and to the right about, when giving point to the right, or to the front.

It will always be observed, as a general rule, in giving point in any direction to the right, left, front, or rear, when charging the enemy, or when opposed singly, man to man, that the point, if against Cavalry, is aimed horizontally, or rather elevated, so as to enter a little above the waist, or on that line, wherever an opening is given; if against Infantry, vertically, to enter the breast, or on that line, according to the same principles.

In giving point to the front against, or when charging, Cavalry, the Lance being in the preparatory Position, " *Guard,*" the point should overpass the horse's head, and be on a line with the ears of a common sized horse, so as to give point horizontally on that line wherever an opening is given.

In giving point to the front against, or when charging, Infantry, the Lance being in the preparatory Position, " *Guard,*" the point should be lowered, and passed close to the horse's nostril and the boss of the bitt, so as to give point vertically on that line, according to the same principles.

In giving point to the right, left, front, or rear, against a retiring enemy, whether Cavalry or Infantry, the point will be aimed either horizontally or vertically, according to circumstances, in any direction, wherever an opening is given.

Exercise and Manœuvres of the Lance.

THE Regiment, Squadron, or Division, being mounted, having taken and proved their distance of ranks and files, and having received the order to come to the Position, " *Carry Lances*," will then receive the preparatory word of command, previous to commencing the Exercise and Manœuvres of the Lance.

WORDS OF COMMAND. MOTIONS.

Prepare to perform Lance Exercise, by Fleugelman.

At this word of command, the Regiment, Squadron, or Division, will remain perfectly steady and attentive, their eyes fixed to the front.

Guard. 1. Lower the right hand so as to seize the Lance in its centre of gravity, or balance ; raise it gently about one inch, and disengage the butt from the boot or bucket ;* the Lance held perfectly steady, and perpendicular.

    2. Let the Lance fall forwards, by casting the butt to the rear ; place it quickly under

---

* The Polish Lancers place the butt on the right foot, behind the stirrup.

WORDS OF COMMAND.	MOTIONS.	
Pl. 5.		the right arm, so that the shaft will remain well closed between the elbow and the body, in nearly a horizontal position, about two inches under the right breast; the back of the hand downwards; the thumb extended upon the Lance, pointing towards the spear; the fingers well closed, encircling the shaft, and the nails uppermost; the point rather elevated, and the butt to the rear, raised about one foot above the horse's croup.
Front give Point. Pl. 6.	1.	Retire the right elbow its whole length to the rear; the arm half extended; the shaft placed under the right breast; if against Cavalry, preserve the horizontal position of the Lance, the point rather elevated; if against Infantry, lower the point vertically to the front.
	2.	Rise gently in the stirrups, bearing the upper part of the body forwards; if against Cavalry, give point with force horizontally to the front, letting the Lance glide along in the hand about three or four

Pl.5.

General, Polish Word of Command, Charge Lances.

Pl.6.

Front Give Point. 1.st Motion.

Pl.7.

Front Give Point. 2.ᵈ Motion.

inches, passing it close to the horse's off ear; the wrist turned inwards; the shaft well closed to the right fore-arm, and supported firmly between it and the body; if against Infantry, give point, vertically, to the front, according to the same principles, passing the Lance close to the horse's nostril, and the boss of the bitt. Having given point, regain the saddle, bring back the Lance immediately to the Position, " *Guard*," and look straight to the front; the body upright.

Pl. 7.

Should the Lancer be attacked on the near side, he will give point to the front, against either Cavalry or Infantry, according to the same principles, in a diagonal direction on that side.

The point may, likewise, be given to the right (or left) of the front, by retiring the right arm its whole length to the rear; if against Cavalry, the shaft placed above the right breast; the point elevated, and clear of the horse's off (or near) ear; if against

H

WORDS OF COMMAND. MOTIONS.

Infantry, the point lowered according to the usual principles. Having given point, regain the saddle, bring back the Lance immediately to the Position, " *Guard*," and look straight to the front; the body upright.

Right give Point. 1.   Retire the right elbow, the arm half extended, and the shaft passed close behind the back : if against Cavalry, preserve the horizontal position of the Lance ; if against Infantry, lower the point, vertically, to the right.

2.   Rise gently in the stirrups, bearing the upper part of the body forwards ; if against Cavalry, give point with force, horizontally, to the right ; the wrist turned to the front ; the fore-finger and the thumb encircling the shaft ; the other three fingers underneath ; the Lance well closed to the right fore-arm, and supported firmly between it and the back ; if against Infantry, give point, vertically and diagonally, to the right, according to the same principles.

Having given point, regain the saddle, bring back the Lance immediately to the Position, " *Guard,*" and look straight to the front ; the body upright.

Left give Point.   1.   Retire the right elbow, the arm half extended ; the spear passed over the horse's head, and the shaft to the front ; if against Cavalry, preserve the horizontal position of the Lance ; if against Infantry, lower the point, vertically, to the left.

2.   Rise gently in the stirrups, bearing the upper part of the body forwards ; if against Cavalry, give point with force, horizontally, to the left ; the wrist close to the body ; the thumb above, and the remaining fingers encircling the shaft ; the Lance well closed under the right fore-arm and the elbow, and rested upon the left fore-arm, near the bend of the elbow ; if against Infantry, give point, vertically and diagonally, to the left, according to the same principles. Having given point, regain the saddle, bring

H 2

WORDS OF COMMAND. MOTIONS.

back the Lance immediately to the Position, " *Guard*," passing it over the horse's head, and look straight to the front ; the body upright.

*By the Right, Reverse Lances.**   1.

Raise the spear of the Lance above the horse's head, so that the point will be on a line with the shade of the cap, and opposite the left eye.

2.

Disengage the shaft from under the right arm, and turn the Lance rapidly, by the right to the rear, between the fore-finger and thumb, the other three fingers closed, so that the point will describe a semicircle ; the shaft grazing the right leg and thigh : if against Cavalry, place the Lance horizontally under the right arm, in the Position, " *Guard*" reversed ; the butt to the front, where the spear was, and on a line with the horse's off ear ; the point to the rear, and the shaft well closed between the right arm and the body ; quit the Lance

Pl. 8.

---

* The words of command may be curtailed to "*Right reverse Lances;*" "*Left reverse Lances,*" &c. &c.

Pl. 8.

By the Right, Reverse Lances.

Pl.9

Rear Give Point (off side) 1.st Motion.

Pl. 10.

Rear Give Point (off side) 2.ᵈ Motion.

WORDS OF COMMAND.	MOTIONS.	
		with the right hand, which reverse, in order to re-seize it; the thumb uppermost; the fingers closed, as laid down in the Position, "*Guard*," and the body upright; if against Infantry, place the Lance vertically; the butt elevated to the front; the point lowered to the rear, and clear of the horse's off flank.
Rear give Point, (Off Side.) Pl. 9.	1.	Extend the right arm its whole length to the front, turning the wrist, at the same time, inwards, so that the hand will be on a line with the chin; the shaft well closed to the right fore-arm; the head turned gently to the right, and the eyes fixed upon the spear.
Pl. 10.	2.	If against Cavalry, give point with force, horizontally, to the rear, by retiring the right arm briskly; if against Infantry, give point, vertically, according to the same principles. Having given point, bring back the Lance immediately to the Position, "*By the Right, reverse Lances,*" and look straight to the front; the body upright.

By the Right,   1.
Rear eighth Point. *

Extend the right arm its whole length to the front, turning the wrist, at the same time, inwards, so that the hand will be on a line with the collar; the butt to the left; the shaft well closed to the right fore-arm; the head turned gently to the right, and the eyes fixed upon the spear.

2.

If against Cavalry, give point with force, horizontally and diagonally, by the right to the rear, by retiring the right arm briskly; if against Infantry, give point, vertically and diagonally, according to the same principles. Having given point, bring back the Lance immediately to the Position, " *By the Right, reverse Lances,*" and look straight to the front; the body upright.

* The strict mathematical principles upon which this Lance Exercise is formed, are thus clearly evinced : the Lancer is conceived to be the centre of a circle, and his Lance the diameter, the different points he gives constitute moving diameters, or radii diverging from that centre, like the needle of the compass, and the circumference of the circle is thereby divided into four quarters, by the right, left, front, and rear points; consequently the radii of the halves of these quarter circles, compose " *Eighth Points,*" and these may be still further subdivided into " *Sixteenth Points,*" whether to the right or left of the front, or to the right or left of the rear.

WORDS OF COMMAND.	MOTIONS.	
Guard.	1.	Raise the socket of the Lance above the horse's head, so that the butt will be on a line with the shade of the cap, and opposite the left eye.*
	2.	Disengage the shaft from under the right arm, and turn the Lance rapidly, with the right hand, from the right to the front, so that the butt will describe a semicircle, and bring back the point to the front; the shaft grazing the right leg and thigh; place the Lance quickly under the right arm, in the Position, " *Guard*," and look straight to the front; the body upright.
By the Left, Reverse Lances.†	1.	Raise the spear of the Lance one foot above the horse's head, disengage

* Should the Lancer have given point against Infantry, and wish to change instantly to the Position, " *Guard*" there is no occasion to return to the first motion, as the butt is sufficiently elevated to resume that of " *Guard*."

† In the Pimlico Exercise, the term, " *Port Lances*" has been most injudiciously chosen in preference to the above word of command, owing, I presume, to a total ignorance of the meaning and derivation of the word *Port*, which properly belongs to another Manœuvre, or Position of the Lance, and will be found hereafter laid down. " *Port Lances*," as also, " *Port Arms*," implies holding the Lance or Musquet in a diagonal position across the body, being derived from the French word, *Porter*, to *bear* or *carry*, which certainly cannot signify, to

WORDS OF COMMAND. MOTIONS.

the shaft from under the right arm, and turn the Lance rapidly, with the right hand, by the left to the rear, so that the point will describe nearly a semicircle ; the spear passing before the body, and over the horse's head ; if against Cavalry, place the Lance, horizontally, on the bend of the left arm ; the butt to the front, on a line with the horse's off ear ; the point to the rear ; the thumb encircling the shaft ; the nails underneath ; the fingers closed, and the body upright ; if against Infantry, place the Lance vertically on, or near, the bend of the left arm ; the butt raised above the horse's head, and over the off ear ; the point lowered to the rear, and clear of the horse's near flank.

WORDS OF COMMAND.	MOTIONS.	
Rear give Point, (*Near Side.*)	1.	Extend the right arm its whole length to the front, so that the hand will be on a

reverse. The French words of command, for such a Position with the Lance or Musquet, are, " *Portez Lances,*" " *Portez Armes.*" I have conformed as much as possible to the words of command adopted for the British Lance Exercise, but in this single instance I am compelled to deviate, and adhere to the original and strictly proper term, and not destroy the beauty of that fine military word of command, " *By the Left, reverse Lances,*" by substituting in its stead, contrary to every rule of propriety and common sense, a term so opposite in its signification, as " *Port Lances.*"

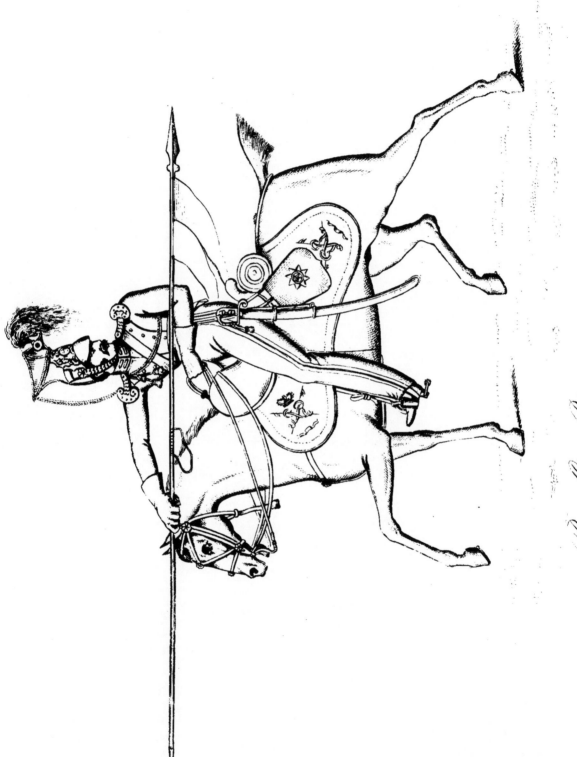

Pl. 11.

Rear Give Point (Near Side) 1st Motion.

Pl.12

Rear Guard (Point (Near Side) 2.d Motion.

WORDS OF COMMAND. MOTIONS. line with the chin; the shaft lightly rested upon the left fore-arm, near the bend of the elbow; the head turned gently to the left, and the eyes fixed upon the spear.

Pl. 11.

2. If against Cavalry, give point with force, horizontally, to the rear, by pushing the right arm briskly; if against Infantry, give point, vertically, according to the same principles. Having given point, bring back the Lance immediately to the Position, " *By the Left, reverse Lances;*" the right wrist drawn near the pit of the stomach; the left hand preserving its proper position, holding the reins, and look straight to the front; the body upright.

Pl. 12.

By the Left, 1. Extend the right arm its whole length
Rear eighth Point. to the front, so that the hand will be on a line with the collar; the butt to the right; the shaft on a line with the horse's off ear, and rested upon the left fore-arm, near the bend of the elbow; the head turned gently to the left, and the eyes fixed upon the spear.

I

2. If against Cavalry, give point with force, horizontally and diagonally, by the left to the rear, by pushing the right arm briskly; if against Infantry, give point, vertically and diagonally, according to the same principles. Having given point, bring back the Lance immediately to the Position, " *By the Left, reverse Lances,*" and look straight to the front; the body upright.

Guard. **1.** Raise the butt of the Lance one foot above the horse's head, disengage the shaft from the left arm, and turn the Lance rapidly, with the right hand, from the left to the front, so that the butt will describe nearly a semicircle, the spear passing before the body and over the horse's head, and bring back the point to the front; place the Lance quickly under the right arm, in the Position, " *Guard,*" and look straight to the front; the body upright.

The Lance being in the Position, " *By the Left, reverse Lances,*" the word of com-

WORDS OF COMMAND. MOTIONS. mand may be given, " *By the Right, reverse Lances.*"*

By the Right,   1.   Raise the butt of the Lance one foot
Reverse Lances.   above the horse's head, disengage the shaft
from the left arm, and turn the Lance
rapidly, with the right hand, from left to
right, changing it briskly from the near to
the off side, so that the point will describe
nearly a circle; the spear passing before
the body and over the horse's head, and
drive the point by the right to the rear;
place the Lance quickly under the right
arm, in the Position, " *By the Right,
reverse Lances,*" ready to give point to the
rear.

The Lance being in the Position, " *By
the Right, reverse Lances,*" the word of command may be given, " *By the Left, reverse
Lances.*"

* Should the Lancer, after having given point on the near side, wish to change instantly to
the Position, " *By the Right, reverse Lances,*" so as to give point on the off side, he will, at
the moment of withdrawing his point, reverse the grasp of the right hand, by a brisk change,
and turn the back of the hand downwards. The point may likewise be given with great effect,
by the left to the rear, on the near side, with the hand reversed, in this position.

60

WORDS OF COMMAND. MOTIONS.

By the Left,
Reverse Lances.   1.

Raise the butt of the Lance one foot above the horse's head; disengage the shaft from under the right arm, and turn the Lance rapidly, with the right hand, from right to left, changing it briskly from the off to the near side, so that the point will describe nearly a circle; the spear passing before the body and over the horse's head, and drive the point by the left to the rear; place the Lance quickly on the bend of the left arm, in the Position, " *By the Left, reverse Lances,*" ready to give point to the rear.

Guard.

As already laid down.

From the St. George, 1.
By the Left,
Reverse Lances.

Incline the spear of the Lance a little to the right, rather elevated; pass the forefinger over the shaft, so that the Lance will be placed between it and the middle finger; drive the spear briskly to the left; disengage the shaft from under the right arm, and swing the Lance twice quickly backwards and forwards over the horse's

Pl. 13.

Pl. 13.

From the S:t George. By the Light. Reverse Lances.

head, to gain the necessary equipoise, or preparatory power; raise it then, with the right hand, above the head, at the full extent of the arm; spin the Lance rapidly round to the right, between the fore and the middle fingers, so that it will describe two or three circles, and bring the point to the front.

2.   Seize the Lance with a firm grasp, lower the right hand, and drive the point by the left to the rear, turning the back of the hand uppermost; place the Lance quickly on the bend of the left arm, in the Position, " *By the Left, reverse Lances,*" according to the principles already laid down, ready to give point to the rear; the nails underneath.

From the St. George, 1.   Incline the butt of the Lance a little to
Guard.   the left; pass the fore-finger over the shaft, so that the Lance will be placed between it and the middle finger; drive the butt briskly to the right; disengage the shaft from the left arm, and swing the Lance

twice quickly backwards and forwards over the horse's head, to gain the necessary equipoise, or preparatory power; raise it then, with the right hand, above the head, at the full extent of the arm; spin the Lance rapidly round to the right, between the fore and the middle fingers, so that it will describe two or three circles, and bring the spear to the front.*

2.   Seize the Lance with a firm grasp, lower the right hand, and wheel the point a full circle round by the right to the rear, close to the right knee, and over the head; place the Lance quickly under the right arm, in the Position " *Guard*," and look straight to the front; the body upright.

The Lance being in the Position, " *By the Left, reverse Lances*," the word of com-

---

* Should the Lancer, when at " *The St. George*," have exceeded the circles required, by a half circle, or otherwise brought the butt to the front, (which he will instantly see by casting a glance of the eye upwards,) he will lower the right hand, and drive the butt a half circle by the right to the rear, close to the right knee, then place the Lance quickly under the right arm, in the Position, " *Guard;*" this is the simplest method, but the one laid down has the finest effect, and is admirable when performed by a highly drilled and expert Lancer.

mand may be given, " *From the St. George, by the Right, reverse Lances.*"

*From the St. George, 1.
By the Right,
Reverse Lances.*

Incline the butt of the Lance a little to the left; the thumb extended, and the remaining fingers encircling the shaft; drive the butt briskly to the right, disengage the shaft from the left arm; and swing the Lance twice quickly backwards and forwards over the horse's head, to gain the necessary equipoise, or preparatory power; raise it then with the right hand above the head, at the full extent of the arm; spin the Lance rapidly round with the right hand, so that it will describe two or three circles, and bring the butt to the front.*

2.   Seize the Lance with a firm grasp, lower the right hand, and wheel the butt a full

---

* Should the Lancer, when at " *The St. George,*" have exceeded the circles required, by a half circle, or otherwise brought the point to the front, he will lower the right hand, and drive the point a half circle by the right to the rear, close to the right knee, then place the Lance quickly under the right arm, in the Position, " *By the Right, reverse Lances,*" ready to give point to the rear.

circle round by the right to the rear, close to the right knee, and over the head; place the Lance quickly under the right arm, in the Position, " *By the Right, reverse Lances,*" according to the principles already laid down, ready to give point to the rear.

The Lance being in the Position, " *By the Right, reverse Lances,*" the word of command may be given, " *From the St. George, by the Left, reverse Lances.*"

From the St. George, 1. *By the Left, Reverse Lances.*

Incline the butt of the Lance a little to the right, rather elevated; the thumb extended, and the remaining fingers encircling the shaft; drive the butt briskly to the right; disengage the shaft from under the right arm, and swing the Lance twice quickly backwards and forwards over the horse's head, to gain the necessary equipoise, or preparatory power; raise it then, with the right hand, above the head, at the full extent of the arm; spin the Lance rapidly round with the right hand, so that

Pl. 14.

Left Parry. Right Gure Point. 1st Motion.

WORDS OF COMMAND. MOTIONS. it will describe two or three circles, and bring the spear to the front.*

2.

Seize the Lance with a firm grasp, lower the right hand, and drive the point by the left to the rear ; place the Lance quickly on the bend of the left arm, in the Position, " *By the Left, reverse Lances;*" the thumb encircling the shaft, and the nails underneath, ready to give point to the rear.

From the St. George, Guard.

As already laid down.

Left Parry, Right give Point.

1.

Pl. 14.

If against Cavalry, parry, horizontally, to the left of the front, the shaft well closed to the right fore-arm and elbow, and bring back the Lance immediately to the Position, " *Guard.*" If against Infantry, raise the point of the Lance about three inches above the horizontal line of the head,

---

* Should the Lancer, when at " *The St. George,*" have exceeded the circles required, by a half circle or otherwise brought the butt to the front, he will lower the right hand, and wheel the butt a full circle round by the left to the rear, close to the left knee and over the head, then place the Lance quickly on the bend of the left arm, in the Position, "*By the Left, reverse Lances;*" the nails underneath, ready to give point to the rear. This is rather a difficult Manœuvre.

K

and a little obliquely to the right; aim a vigorous oblique stroke of the Lance to the left, by carrying the spear from top to bottom, from above the horse's head, rather grazing his near shoulder, and sweeping the point round to the left, so as to parry the bayonet, or give a severe cut on the head, arms, or breast. Having parried, bring back the Lance immediately to the Position, " *Guard*."

Pl. 15.

2.   Retire the right elbow, the arm half extended; the butt passed behind the back, and the shaft to the rear; if against Cavalry, preserve the horizontal position of the Lance; if against Infantry, lower the point, vertically, to the right.

3.   Rise gently in the stirrups, bearing the upper part of the body forwards; if against Cavalry, give point with force, horizontally, to the right, according to the principles already laid down; if against Infantry, give point, vertically and diagonally, to the right, according to the same principles.

Pl. 15.

Left Parry. Right Give Point. 2.ᵈ Motion.

WORDS OF COMMAND. MOTIONS.

Having given point, regain the saddle, bring back the Lance immediately to the Position, " *Guard*," and look straight to the front ; the body upright.

Right Parry,
Left give Point.

1.

If against Cavalry, parry, horizontally, to the right of the front ; the shaft well closed to the right fore-arm and elbow, and bring back the Lance immediately to the Position, " *Guard ;*" if against Infantry, raise the point of the Lance about three inches above the horizontal line of the head, and a little obliquely to the left ; aim a vigorous oblique stroke of the Lance to the right, by carrying the spear from top to bottom, from above the horse's head, passing it close to his off shoulder, and sweeping the point round to the right, so as to parry the bayonet, or give a severe cut on the head, arms, or breast. Having parried, bring back the Lance immediately to the Position, " *Guard.*"

2.

Retire the right elbow, the arm half extended ; the spear passed over the horse's

K 2

head, and the shaft to the front ; if against Cavalry, preserve the horizontal position of the Lance ; if against Infantry, lower the point, vertically, to the left.

3.   Rise gently in the stirrups, bearing the upper part of the body forwards ; if against Cavalry, give point with force, horizontally, to the left, according to the principles already laid down ; if against Infantry, give point, vertically and diagonally, to the left, according to the same principles. Having given point, regain the saddle, bring back the Lance immediately to the Position, " *Guard*," and look straight to the front ; the body upright.

Right and Left Parry, 1.   If against Cavalry, parry, horizontally, to
Front give Point.   the right, and then to the left, of the front ; the shaft well closed to the right fore-arm and elbow, and bring back the Lance immediately to the Position, " *Guard ;*" if against Infantry, raise the point of the Lance about three inches above the horizontal line of the head, and a little ob-

liquely to the left; aim a vigorous oblique stroke of the Lance to the right, and then to the left, by recovering the Lance, and carrying the spear from top to bottom, from above the horse's head, passing it close, first to his off, and then to his near, shoulder, and sweeping the point round to the right, and then to the left, so as to parry the bayonet, or give a severe cut on the head, arms, or breast. Having parried on both sides of the front, bring back the Lance immediately to the Position, " *Guard.*"

2. Retire the right elbow its whole length to the rear; the arm half extended; the shaft placed under the right breast; if against Cavalry, preserve the horizontal position of the Lance, the point rather elevated; if against Infantry, lower the point vertically to the front.

3. Rise gently in the stirrups, bearing the upper part of the body forwards; if against Cavalry, give point with force, horizontally, to the front, according to the principles.

WORDS OF COMMAND. MOTIONS. already laid down; if against Infantry, give point, vertically, to the front, according to the same principles. Having given point, regain the saddle, bring back the Lance immediately to the Position, "*Guard*," and look straight to the front; the body upright.

Left and Right Parry, 1. *Front give Point.* If against Cavalry, parry, horizontally, to the left, and then to the right, of the front; the shaft well closed to the right fore-arm and elbow, and bring back the Lance immediately to the Position, " *Guard;*" if against Infantry, raise the point of the Lance about three inches above the horizontal line of the head, and a little obliquely to the right; aim a vigorous oblique stroke of the Lance, first to the left, and then to the right, by recovering the Lance, and carrying the spear from top to bottom from above the horse's head, passing it close, first to his near, and then to his off, shoulder, sweeping the point round to the left, and then to the right, so as to parry the bayonet, or give a severe cut on the

WORDS OF COMMAND. MOTIONS. head, arms, or breast. Having parried on both sides of the front, bring back the Lance immediately to the Position, "*Guard.*"

2. 3.　　As already laid down.

Round Parry,　1.　This motion being against Cavalry, in-
Front give Point.*　cline the spear of the Lance to the extreme right, keeping the shaft high and firm under the right arm, and sweep the Lance, rapidly and horizontally, round from the right to the rear of the left side, over the horse's head, in a circular manner, twisting the upper part of the body at the same time with the motion, so that the point will describe a semicircle; the shaft well closed to the right fore-arm and elbow; bring back the Lance quickly to the first Position, and repeat the same motion a second and third time. Having parried thrice round, bring back the Lance imme-diately to the Position, " *Guard.*"

* The Polish word of command implies, " *Round-about Parry.*" The French word is, " *Alentour Paréz,*" which has the same signification.

WORDS OF COMMAND. MOTIONS.
2. 3.

As already laid down.

The point may likewise be given, in all these manœuvres, to the right, or left, and to the rear, in any direction, against either Cavalry or Infantry, wherever the exigency of the moment may require it, according to the principles already laid down, under the heads of " *Right*," " *Left*," and " *Rear give Point.*"

Round Parry,
From the St. George,
By the Left,
Reverse Lances.

This Manœuvre being supposed to be against Cavalry in front, and Cavalry or Infantry to the rear, will be executed according to the principles already laid down under their several heads. The point may then be given, " *To the Rear,*" or " *An Eighth, or a Sixteenth, to the Rear,*" according to circumstances, as already laid down.

From the St. George,
Guard.

As already laid down.

Carry Lances. 1.

Raise the Lance briskly with the right hand; place the butt in the boot or bucket, attached to the off stirrup, and raise the right hand on a line with the shoulder; the elbow about eight inches from the shaft; the thumb in the sling; the fingers closed, and the Lance held perfectly perpendicular; the body upright.

The Regiment, Squadron, or Division, having closed their ranks and files, according to order, and being aligned and dressed, if the Commanding Officer's intention is not to dismount them, may then receive the order, to come to the Position, " *Sling*," or to that of " *Rest Lances*," and " *Sit at Ease.*"

General Observations.

SUPPOSING Lancers to be acting as Skirmishers, or to be engaged singly, the foregoing manœuvres are intended to furnish them both with the means of attack and defence, as follow:

Should the Lancer be attacked on his right, or left, by Cavalry, he must parry the cuts made at him by a round-about or circular horizontal motion of his Lance; after which he will give point, horizontally, wherever an opening is given. If he is attacked, in either case, by Infantry, he should attack likewise, either by giving point with vigour, or by a severe oblique cut from top to bottom, from above the horse's head, so as to parry the thrusts of the bayonet, or wound his adversary on the head, arms, or breast. This oblique cut, or parry, should instantly be followed up by giving point vigorously, according to circumstances, wherever his enemy, if either (or both) Cavalry or Infantry, is most exposed. The mode of Defence is laid down under the several heads of " *Right*," " *Left*," and " *Round Parry*," and that of attack by giving point, or by the oblique cut of the Lance. The " *Round Parry*" may likewise be given with as much effect with the butt to the front, when in the Position, " *By the Right, reverse Lances.*"

In the round-about or circular, and horizontal, motions of the Lance, it is indispensably necessary that the Lancer takes particular care never to remove the Lance from his right fore-arm. The elbow, in these motions, should always remain firmly closed upon the shaft.

In changing from one parry to another, or in turning the Lance round on any occasion, the Lancers must take the greatest care not to raise the Lance too high above the horse's head, or the butt will strike against his haunches, and create confusion.

It must be particularly instilled into the minds of the Lancers, that the moment the point is given, in any direction, it must in every instance be immediately withdrawn; likewise, that the point is invariably given against the antagonist in preference to the horse, except against a retiring enemy, when the point may be given against either one or the other. The reason is thus obvious: in the attack, the adversary's horse, in advancing and receiving the point, will still rush further on it, and if not instantly disengaged, will either shiver the Lance in pieces, or the conflicting shock itself may unhorse the Lancer, whereas in retiring, the horse, on receiving the point, gallops from it, and thus frees himself from the Lance.

In giving point, " *By the Left, to the Rear*," against either Cavalry or Infantry in close action, the butt of the Lance should be extended to the front at the same time with the right arm; but when the adversary is at a greater distance than the half-length of the Lance, the hand should be shifted to the full extent of the arm along the shaft, and as near the butt as it will reach, by a quick motion, the right shoulder well brought up, previous to giving point; and on its being given, the Lance must be withdrawn, and re-grasped instantly in its proper balance, otherwise the weight of the spear and bandrol will overbalance the Lance, and endanger the safety of the Lancer.

In rising in the stirrups to give point, it is essential that the Lancer does not lose his balance, or derange his seat, by reason of the frequent exertions and motions he is obliged to make in wielding the Lance, as Infantry might take advantage of it, and, by closing with him, attempt to unhorse him by seizing him by the leg or foot.

The foregoing manœuvres, combined with many others, may be executed as laid down under their several heads, changing them alternately, as the Commanding Officer may think proper, varying them at his pleasure, and exercising the Lancers frequently in their practice. When once a Regiment is perfectly drilled, so as fully to comprehend the different motions and positions required to perform each manœuvre, the Lance Exercise on Horseback may be performed at a gallop, and in speed, in the same manner as the Sword Exercise; and as the manœuvres and evolutions of both these arms are as nearly assimilated as possible, the drill and instruction for the one and the other will equally tend towards improvement and perfection in both.

The Lance Exercise on Foot, for preliminary instruction, is equally as easy as it is on Horseback, as well for those who command, as for the Lancers themselves. Faults can then be more easily perceived, and may be corrected with more accuracy. The Exercise on Foot is to be executed, in every respect, according to the same principles, and the same words of command are to be made use of, as for the Lance Exercise on Horseback.

Pl.16.

Trail Lances.

Escorts and Honors.

WHEN in Line, or in Column, or for the Escort of his Majesty, or the Royal Family, and for receiving, or lodging, the Standards, or other duties of Honor, when mounted, the Lances being previously in the Position, " *Carry Lances*," the order may be given to come to that of " *Trail Lances*," as follows:

WORDS OF COMMAND.	MOTIONS.	
Trail Lances.	1.	RAISE the Lance gently about one inch, and disengage the butt from the boot or bucket; the Lance held perfectly steady and perpendicular.
Pl. 16.	2.	Lower the Lance to the left, so that it will take a diagonal Position; the spear upwards, to the left, and to the front; the butt downwards, to the right, and to the rear; the right hand resting upon the thick part of the thigh; the fingers closed, and the nails underneath.

DISMOUNTING

AND

FILING.

PART IV.

𝔇𝔦𝔰𝔪𝔬𝔲𝔫𝔱𝔦𝔫𝔤.

AFTER the Lance Exercise on Horseback is performed, and the Commanding Officer's intention is to dismount the Lancers, the Regiment, Squadron, or Division, having previously formed line, and the ranks being at " *Close Order*," the word of command will be given for that purpose, always establishing it as a general rule, that the Lances must be brought to the Position, " *Carry Lances*," previous to the order being given to Dismount.

Prepare to
Dismount.

1.

THE left files will rein back, according to order; the whole of the Lancers will then lower the right hand on the Lance, to the full extent of the arm, upon a line with the knee, and disengage the butt from the boot or bucket, by raising it about three inches; the Lance held perfectly steady and perpendicular.

2.

Raise the Lance, perpendicularly, with a brisk motion of the right hand, throwing it, at the same time, upwards, so as to grasp the shaft within eighteen inches of the butt.

3.

Pass the butt about four inches above the horse's neck, close to the front of the saddle, from the off to the near side, between the reins and the neck, under the bridle hand, which will, for a moment, support the Lance without lowering it; let the Lance glide obliquely of itself through the left hand under the reins, so that the butt will be about eight or ten inches from the ground; seize a lock of the horse's

WORDS OF COMMAND. MOTIONS. mane with the right hand, and twist it round the thumb of the left, in the same manner as in mounting, without letting go the Lance or the reins; the point kept well upwards;* place the right hand upon the off holster, the thumb within, the remaining fingers without, and disengage the right foot from the stirrup.

Dismount. 1. Rise upon the near stirrup, supporting the weight of the body, for a moment, with the hands upon the pommel of the saddle; pass the right leg, well extended, gently over the horse's croup, without touching it, and shift the right hand, at the same time, from the pommel to the cantle of the saddle; pause an instant; dismount gently, and bring the right foot to the ground first; the body upright; both heels closed and upon the same line; quit the reins and the horse's mane with the left hand, letting the butt touch the ground on quit-

---

*The greatest attention possible must be paid by the Lancers, both in mounting and dismounting, to keep the point of the Lance well upwards in this position, in order to prevent the butt from striking against, or even touching, the horses next in the ranks, which circumstance generally creates the greatest confusion, and will sometimes pervade a whole Troop or Squadron.

ting the near stirrup; face to the left; advance one pace to the front; seize the near bridon rein, about two inches from the bitt, with the right hand, and bring the Lance at the same time to the Position, " *Carry Lances,*" with the left hand, on that side.

Left Files, Front Form. March.

At the word, " *March,*" the left files will advance, and lead their horses into the intervals of their respective ranks; the whole of the Lancers will then receive the order to come to the Position, "*Rest Lances,*" with the left hand on that side, preparatory to receiving the word, " *Stand at Ease.*"

Stand at Ease.

According to order; or the word, " *Stand at Ease,*" may be given when at the Position, " *Carry Lances,*" without any intermediate word of command.

The Lancers will likewise be practised in dismounting at the off side, which will correspond precisely with the rules laid down for the near side, with the difference, that

WORDS OF COMMAND. MOTIONS. the Lance, reins, and horse's mane, are to be well grasped with the right hand, and the sword is to be previously raised up with the left hand and laid across in front, under the reins, on the thighs, the point to the right; and the left leg, in dismounting, is to be passed, well extended, over the horse's croup. The trifling motions to be reversed, will naturally and instantaneously point themselves out to the Lancers.

The Regiment, Squadron, or Division will be frequently drilled to dismount in an open Column of six deep, which will be executed as follows, the Lancers having previously formed Line, and the Ranks being at " *Close Order :*"

WORDS OF COMMAND.

From the Right of Threes,
To the Front File.

March.

THE right files of ranks by threes, belonging to the front rank, will disengage themselves, by advancing clear of the line.

At the word, " *March,*" the whole of the Lancers belonging to both ranks will successively advance, dressing by the right or centre, according to order; the centre and left files of ranks by threes, belonging

M 2

to the front rank, will, while advancing, double behind, and follow the right files; after which, the right, centre, and left files, belonging to the rear rank, will successively double behind and follow them; the column thus formed, will cover correctly, and take open distance of one horse's length upon the march.

Halt, Dress.

The commanding officer will give the word, " *Halt, Dress,*" after the column has advanced a short distance, when he sees that the files cover correctly, and that they have taken their proper distance, preparatory to receiving the order to dismount.

Prepare to Dismount.

According to order, as already laid down.

The Regiment, Squadron, or Division, will, when ready to mount, receive orders to " *Stand to their Horses,*" " *Carry Lances,*"* " *Prepare to Mount,*" and " *Mount,*" as already laid down; and will

---

* The Lancers may be instructed to come to the Position, " *Carry Lances,*" at the word, " *Stand to your Horses,*" without giving that preparatory word of command.

resume its proper formation at either a walk, trot, or gallop, in the following manner :

WORDS OF COMMAND. *Front form Line, or Squadron. March.*	THE right files of ranks by threes, belonging to both ranks, will stand fast; the centre and left files will advance from column, form line, and dress by the pivots.
Rear Rank, close Order. March.	The rear rank will close to the front, to within half a horse's length, in the usual manner.
	The Regiment, Squadron, or Division, being aligned and dressed, may then receive the order to come to the Position, " *Sling,*" or to that of " *Rest Lances,*" and " *Sit at Ease.*"

Filing.

THE Regiment, Squadron, or Division, being dismounted, previous to filing off to their quarters or stables, and the Lancers having come to the Position, " *Carry Lances*," with the left hand, on that side, the word of command will be given to change to that of " *Shoulder Lances.*"

WORDS OF COMMAND. MOTIONS.

*Shoulder Lances.** 1. QUIT the Lance with the left hand ; let it fall from the Position, " *Carry Lances*," when " *Standing to Horse*," into the hollow of the left shoulder, and hook up the sword upon the sword-belt.

2. Re-seize the Lance with the left hand, about two feet from the butt ; the hand reversed ; the thumb above upon the shaft the fingers underneath ; the Lance held in a diagonal Position ; the shaft rested upon the left shoulder ; the butt raised about six inches from the ground, inclined rather forwards, and the spear to the rear.

Right or Left File. According to order.
March.

Should any obstacle prevent the Lancers from filing to the right, or left, when on

* The Polish word implies, " *Slope Lances.*"

WORDS OF COMMAND. MOTIONS. the near side of their horses ; in that case they will change to the off side, by passing before the horse's head, and prepare to lead them with the left hand, first shifting the Lance from the left into the right hand, and coming to the Position, " *Shoulder Lances*," on the right side, as already laid down. The trifling motions to be reversed will naturally and instantaneously point themselves out to the Lancers.

INSPECTION

OF

ARMS.

PART V.

Lances.

WHEN the Officer Commanding the Regiment, Squadron, or Division, makes an inspection of Lances, the Lancers will be formed in a rank entire, or single rank, in column of Troops, or Divisions; they will then receive orders to come to the Position, " *Guard,*" and afterwards to that of " *By the Right, reverse Lances,*" should he not go round by the rear. The first motion will enable him to observe whether the spear, bandrol, bandlets, and sling, are in good order; and the latter to examine the butt, and the socket of the butt.

Pistols.

WHEN an inspection of Pistols takes place, the Lances being previously in the Position, " *Carry Lances,*" the Lancers will receive the order to come to that of " *Sling Lances,*" on the left, (or right,) arm, or to the Position, " *Secure Lances,*" as follows :

WORDS OF COMMAND.	MOTIONS.	
(Left Arm,) *Sling Lances.*	1.	LOWER the right hand on the Lance, to the full extent of the arm, upon a line with the knee, and disengage the butt from the boot or bucket, by raising it about three inches; the Lance held perfectly steady and perpendicular.
	2.	Raise the Lance perpendicularly, with a brisk motion of the right hand, throwing it, at the same time, upwards, so as to grasp the shaft within eighteen inches of the butt.
	3.	Pass the butt over the bridle hand, from the off to the near side; let the Lance

glide through the right hand, perpendicularly, downwards, and place the butt in the boot or bucket attached to the near stirrup; place both hands near each other; quit the reins with the left hand, making sure of them with the right, and change the Lance at the same moment into the left hand; the thumb in the sling.

4. Pass the left arm quickly through the sling, and cast the Lance to the rear with a brisk motion of the right hand, so that it will hang about midway between the elbow and the shoulder, taking care not to disturb the horse's mouth; re-seize the reins then with the left hand,* lengthen them with the right; unbuckle the winding strap, and throw back the schabraque.

Draw Pistols. 1. Draw the Pistol from the holster, and bring it to the recover; the muzzle in the air; present it for inspection, according

---

* Should the Lancers not prepare to " *Draw Pistols,*" the right hand will afterwards fall behind the thigh.

WORDS OF COMMAND. MOTIONS.

to order; after which, without waiting for any word of command, return the Pistol; replace the schabaque; re-buckle the winding strap, and take up the reins.

Carry Lances. 1. Seize the reins with the right hand, and quit them with the left; drive the Lance forward with a brisk motion of the left arm; support it gently with the right thumb, without letting go the reins; grasp the shaft with the left hand reversed, which will slide upwards, and disengage the left arm from the sling.

2. Re-seize the reins with the left hand, bringing the hands close to each other, and supporting the Lance for a moment with the left thumb, and quit them with the right; seize the Lance, at the same time, with the right hand, at the full extent of the arm, between the reins and the horse's neck.

3. Raise the Lance, perpendicularly, with a brisk motion of the right hand, out of the

WORDS OF COMMAND. MOTIONS. left boot or bucket, throwing it, at the same time, upwards ; pass the butt about four inches over the horse's neck, close to the front of the saddle, from the near to the off side ; let the Lance glide, perpendicularly, downwards, through the right hand ; place the butt in the boot or bucket attached to the off stirrup, and raise the right hand on a line with the shoulder ; the elbow about eight inches from the shaft ; the thumb in the sling ; the fingers closed, and the Lance held perfectly perpendicular.

Secure Lances. 1. Lower the right hand on the Lance to the full extent of the arm, upon a line with the knee, and disengage the butt from the boot or bucket, by raising it about three inches ; the Lance held perfectly steady and perpendicular.

2. Raise the Lance, perpendicularly, with the right hand ; pass the butt under the right thigh, and lower the Lance so that the butt will be placed rather below the

point of the right foot; support the Lance with the knee, and dispose of it in such a manner, that the shaft will be rested against the left shoulder, in a diagonal position, across the body; the spear upwards, to the left, and the butt downwards, to the right; lengthen the reins then with the right hand; unbuckle the winding strap, and throw back the schabraque.

Pl. 17.

Draw Pistols.

According to order, after inspection, without waiting for any words of command, return the pistol; replace the schabraque; re-buckle the winding strap; take up the reins; replace the Lance in the boot or bucket attached to the off stirrup, and resume the Position, " *Carry Lances.*"

Pl.17.

𝔖𝔴𝔬𝔯𝔡𝔰.

WHEN an inspection of Swords takes place, the Lances being previously in the Position, " *Carry Lances*," the Lancers will receive the order to come to that of " *Sling Lances*," on the left arm, as already laid down.

WORDS OF COMMAND. MOTIONS.

Draw Swords.   1.   DIRECT the eyes to the Sword-hilt, bringing the right hand, with a quick motion, across the body, and over the bridle arm, to the sword-knot; place it upon the wrist, and turn the hand twice inwards, to make it fast; seize the hilt at the same time, the back of the hand to the rear, and look to the right Fleugelman for the second motion.

2.   Draw the Sword from the scabbard with the full extent of the arm ; sink the right hand, at the same time, till the hilt is immediately under the chin, the blade perpendicular, and the back of the hand outwards.

WORDS OF COMMAND.   MOTIONS.

3.

Lower the hilt on a line with the bridle hand, the elbow near the body, the blade perpendicular, and the wrist in a small degree rounded, turning the edge inwards, in the direction of the horse's left ear, which completes the Position, " *Carry Swords.*"

Slope Swords.   1.

From the Position, " *Carry Swords,*" distend the second, third, and fourth fingers from the gripe of the sword, so that the back of the blade will fall into, and meet the hollow of, the right shoulder, which will support it, the edge directed to the front, the sword kept perfectly steady at whatever pace the horse may be moving.

Carry Swords.   1.

Resume the Position of the third motion of " *Draw Swords.*"

Return Swords.   1.

From the Position, " *Carry Swords,*" bring the Sword-hilt quickly to the hollow of the left shoulder ; the back of the hand outwards, and the blade perfectly perpendicular; drop the blade, (but not the hand,) without pausing, to the rear, close by the left shoulder, directing the eyes to the scabbard, and resting the blade upon the bridle-arm ; return the Sword immediately into the scabbard,* until the hand and elbow are in a line with each other, square across the body, keeping the back of the hand directed to the rear.

2.   Drive the sword, quickly, full into the scabbard, and loosen the Sword-knot instantly from the wrist, keeping the hand upon the hilt, and look to the Fleugelman for the motion to carry the right hand quickly from the hilt to the off side.

Carry Lances.   As already laid down.

The Position, " *Sling Lances,*" on the left arm, or that of " *Secure Lances,*" will likewise be made use of for the inspection

---

* In Regiments of Lancers, the front sling of the Sword-belt should be very short, in order that the Sword may not be obstructed, in returning it, by the Position of the Lance when slung upon the left arm.

WORDS OF COMMAND. MOTIONS. of Carbines, if used ;* and the latter Position when charging Carbines, or Pistols, at a halt, when acting as Skirmishers.

* In the Polish Regiments of Lancers, an equal proportion of each Troop were armed with Carbines, in consequence of which I have attended to the rules to be observed relative to that arm when skirmishing.

SKIRMISHERS.

PART VI.

Preliminary Instructions.

SKIRMISHERS, or Ranks detached to fire, should be at least two hundred yards from the Regiment or Squadron, if the ground will allow it. When any part of the Squadron is detached to attack, or fire, the remainder will always support, with their Lances in the Position, " *Carry*," or in that of " *Trail Lances*," preparatory to changing them to that required for the attack. The Standard always remains with the body of the Squadron, and never moves with any detached part of it. Single Skirmishers can always take the surest aim, with their Carbines or Pistols, to the left; they will also occasionally fire to the front, and to the right, but must take the greatest care not to hit or burn the horse's head, or at that time to spur him. The Skirmishers should always retire in proportion as the Regiment or Squadron retires; cover the front of it at one hundred and fifty yards distance at least, and manage so as to keep up a constant fire; nor should they ever remain in a cluster, to become a mark. All firings are best performed on the move, and it is unnecessary to halt for that purpose only. Whenever the Line retires, the Skirmishers should be ordered to cover the Retreat, and should join at the first signal. No Skirmishers are ever to fire but when advanced to the front, and never when behind other men. If not ordered to join, the Skirmishers will retire through the intervals, when the Line advances to charge, and will form and support. The Retreat of the Line should be generally made at a brisk pace, to get quick off the ground, and no time ought to be lost in giving the proper signal, or word of command. In detached open ranks, the Officer commanding the Rank is always most conveniently placed in the centre of it, and the Skirmishers dress, and are directed by him.

The Skirmishers are to be very attentive and alert in instantly obeying the signals made for their direction, particularly those of ceasing to fire, and of rallying to their Divisions, and when the signal for calling in Skirmishers is succeeded by that of " *Rally,*" made from the main body; the Divisions themselves will return quickly, even though they should not then be joined by their detached men.

When Lancers are employed to act as Skirmishers, the Lance being previously in the Position, " *Carry Lances,*" they may be directed to come to that of " *Sling Lances,*" on the left arm, as already laid down, or accustomed to change alternately from the Carbine, or Pistol, to the Lance, by bringing the latter to the Position, " *Port Lances,*" as follows, in order to enable them to make use of their fire-arms :

WORDS OF COMMAND.	MOTIONS.	
*Port Lances.**	1.	LOWER the right hand so as to seize the Lance rather below the middle, and disengage the butt from the boot or bucket, by raising it about three inches; the Lance held perfectly steady and perpendicular.
	2.	Change the Lance into the left hand, without quitting the reins, letting it glide obliquely of itself through the hand to

* This is the proper Position, referred to in a former note, page 55. The French word of command is, " *En tirailleurs Portez Lances,*" meaning thereby, to carry Lances as Skirmishers, in order to distinguish it from, " *Portez Lances,*" it being a different Position.—— The English Language, more copious in translations, and fertile in expressing the sense, can afford to translate the former Word of Command simply into " *Port Lances,*" without prefixing any preparatory word; and the latter into " *Carry Lances,*" as has been already done with respect to " *Carry Arms,*" " *Port Arms.*"—The Polish word of command has the same signification as the French.

Pl. 18.

its proper balance, and dispose of it in such a manner that it will be held in a diagonal Position across the body; the spear upwards, to the left, and the butt downwards, to the right. When ready, unstrap the Carbine, or unbuckle the winding strap; throw back the schabraque, and draw the Pistol from the holster; load, and come to the recover; the muzzle in the air. Having fired, without waiting for any words of command, re-load, strap up, or sling the Carbine, or return the Pistol, and replace the schabraque, without re-buckling the winding strap; re-seize the Lance then with the right hand, quit it with the left, and bring it immediately to the Position, " *Guard.*"

The Lance being previously in the Position, " *Guard,*" or in that of " *Trail Lances,*" may likewise be changed alternately to that of " *Port,*" or " *Secure Lances,*" according to the rules laid down for the second motion under their several heads, in order to enable the Lancers to fire and re-load.

Pl.18.

Port Lances.

General Rules for Skirmishing.

WHEN the Commanding Officer wishes to exercise the Lancers to act and disperse themselves as Skirmishers, to cover the front of the Regiment, or Squadron, he will direct Flank Divisions, or Sub-Divisions, to be previously warned for that duty. The Officers, or Non-commissioned Officers, commanding the named Divisions, having received such orders, will advance to the front, and give the word of command as follows:

WORDS OF COMMAND.

Right (or Left) Division, (or Sub-Divisions,) Attention.
As Skirmishers, To the Front. March.

AT the word, " *March*," the named Divisions, or Sub-Divisions, will advance rapidly about one hundred and fifty yards in front of their respective Squadrons; and the Officers, or Non-commissioned Officers, commanding them will, immediately on disengaging, give the word, " *Right (or Left) Incline*," according to the flank they advance from, in order to gradually gain, and exactly arrive, on a line with the centre of their Squadrons on the March; having accomplished which, they will immediately give the word, " *Forward*," and move straight to the front. From this body there will be detached a Sub-Division, or three or more files belonging to each Division, one hundred yards still farther forwards, where they will halt fronting the enemy. The outward flank files of this advanced Detachment will stand fast, while the others, dispersing themselves as Skirmishers, file inwards towards each other, in order to divide the ground, and extend themselves so as to take up their interval, which cannot be positively fixed, but will depend upon the number of Lancers acting as Skirmishers, and the extent of the front of the Regiment or Squadron; and in the first case they will, of course, be more numerous; the Lancers will then skirmish with their Carbines, or Pistols, or manœuvre with their Lances, and at the same time cover the front of the Reserve as well as that of the Regiment or Squadron. This operation, followed by all the Detachments from the Squadrons, will effectually cover the front of the Corps by completely outflanking the Wings.

In this situation the advanced line of Skirmishers will bring their Lances immediately to the Position, " *Guard*," should they not be otherwise ordered to make use of their Carbines or Pistols; in either of which cases, they are to bring them to the " *Recover*," and come to the Position, " *Sling Lances*," on the left arm, or support them with the left hand, without letting go the reins, in that of " *Port Lances*," so as to enable them to fire, and afterwards change to that of " *Secure Lances*," in order to re-load, as already laid down. After strapping up, or slinging their Carbines, or returning their Pistols, the Lancers will immediately resume the Position, "*Guard*," while advancing, or fronting; and those of the rear rank will invariably cover their front rank files, while the front rank advances in skirmishing.

When the front rank has fired, the rear rank will be brought forward successively in its turn by the Officer or Non-commissioned Officer who is stationed between the two lines, in order to see and direct the rear one. The advancing line will regulate its pace by his, and will halt and dress by him when he halts. For this movement of the rear line to the front, the Officer or Non-commissioned Officer commanding will give the word, "*Rear Rank, Forward*," accompanied by a wide signal with his Sword. The rear rank will pass the front line fifty yards; when passed, the rear line begins to load.

In order to prevent the mistakes which frequently occur in giving the word of command verbally to Troops acting as Skirmishers, where it is impossible the voice can be heard at such a distance as the extent which is to be covered, the trumpet or bugle should always be made use of in addition, to express all the necessary words of command.

The files of the front line must attend particularly to the circumstance of not firing until the rear line (their support) is loaded,

P

On this principle will each rank pass through the other, successively firing and supporting each other.

Each Lancer of the front rank, either in advancing or retiring, will pass his rear rank file on his right, while the rear rank Lancers, under the same circumstances, will pass on the left. This regulation prevents any two Lancers from passing through the same interval.

When the Regiment or Squadron retires, the retreat will be sounded, and the Skirmishers will retire *en echiquier*, in the following manner:—When the rank next the enemy has fired, it will wheel "*Left About*," and retire by word of command, assisted by signal, and sound of trumpet or bugle. The Lancers will then return their Carbines or Pistols, if using them, and will immediately, and always while retiring, bring their Lances to the Position, "*By the Right, reverse Lances*," and form fifty yards in the rear of those by whom they were before covered, by fronting "*Right About*," and resuming the Position, "*Guard*," while fronting; but if ordered to make use of their Carbines or Pistols, they will, as they pass, immediately begin to load. The instant the retiring line has arrived within ten yards of the supporting one, the latter will receive orders to advance just sufficiently to clear it, and give confidence to the former; and when the retiring line has passed it, the Skirmishers of the supporting one, which will then become the front line, will make a flank movement to each hand for a few paces, and back again, in order not to be fixed marks for the enemy's Skirmishers; at the same time they are occasionally to halt, and fire, as they perceive their rear file loaded. The Skirmishers of the rear rank will retire in the same manner through the intervals of the front rank, by wheeling " *Left About*," also, and will form fifty yards in the rear of it, going through the different motions of the Lance already pointed out for the front rank, and so on, alternately, as long as the Regiment or Squadron retires. Thus the too lines will retire through each other, successively fronting and supporting. To retire, the word of command is, " *About ;*" to face the enemy, " *Front.*" In retiring, each Lancer will wheel his horse to the " *Left About ;*" in fronting, he brings him to the " *Right About.*"

When the Regiment or Squadron regains its original position, or whenever the Skirmishers are intended to be recalled, the " *Call-in Skirmishers* " will be sounded. At this signal, the Lancers will retire, and form to the Reserve, previous to gaining the rear of the Regiment or Squadron, and entering into their places in line; they will then, without waiting for any words of command, strap up their Carbines, or return their Pistols, if using them ; and in all cases bring their Lances to the Position, " *Carry*," or to that of " *Trail Lances.*" The Officers or Non-commissioned Officers commanding the Divisions or Sub-Divisions, will put them about by threes, and return to their posts in Squadron ; but should the line be advancing to the charge, the Divisions or Sub-Divisions, if they can, will gain their places in Squadron, and join in the charge, or otherwise they will form behind the Regiment or Squadron, and support.

When a halt is sounded, the Skirmishers will halt, and observe all the movements of the Regiment or Squadron, to conform to them. When a line or column moves to a flank, and that Skirmishers are out, they are not to wait an order for them to conform to that movement of the main body, but will wheel in such direction so as to place themselves in front of, and cover, that flank which may be exposed to the enemy, and will bring their Lances to the Position, " *Carry*," or to that of " *Trail Lances*," until they have arrived at their destination : for instance, if the movement of the line is to the right, then to the left of the line of march must be covered, and the reverse is to be observed in the opposite case.

The Skirmishers covering a flank movement will march in single file. The rear rank Lancer immediately behind his front rank file, judging the distance so as completely to cover the Regiment or Squadron, which should be out-flanked by its Skirmishers rather than otherwise, the same principle of reserving the fire with the front line, until the rear support is loaded, must equally be attended to in flank movements, as in the cases of advancing or retiring ; but in the practice there is this difference, that a front file, in a flank movement, cannot see when the reserve has loaded, therefore it is to be announced to him by the word " *Ready*," when he will fire at discretion.

As Skirmishers are frequently placed in very difficult situations, where it is impossible that an Officer or Non-commissioned Officer can always be present to attend to them, and enforce a strict observance to, and execution of, this most essential and important branch of their duty, it will be advisable in such cases to select, if possible, for this purpose, the most steady and intelligent Lancers that can be picked out, who will be able to act of themselves upon all occasions, and take advantage of any unforeseen circumstances which may occur.

MANŒUVRES

AND

EVOLUTIONS.

PART VII.

𝕲eneral 𝕴nstructions.

THE Manœuvres and Evolutions of Regiments of Lancers will be entirely the same, and in every respect conformable to those fixed in His Majesty's Instructions and Regulations for the Formations and Movements of the Cavalry.

When marching in line, and in every other march, in order of battle, or at the moment of charging Cavalry, when the Officer commanding the Regiment, Squadron, or Division, gives the preparatory order for the attack, the whole of the Lancers belonging to the front rank will bring their Lances to the horizontal Position, " *Guard*," the spear over-passing the horse's head, and on a line with his off ear, so as to enter a little above the waist. When charging Infantry, the Lancers will come to the vertical position, the spear on a line with the boss of the bitt, so as to pass close to the horse's nostril, and enter the breast. The rear rank will, in all these cases, instead of coming to the horizontal or vertical Position, only lower their Lances by inclining them sufficiently forwards, so that the point will be on a line with the tops of the caps of the front rank, or they may receive orders to " *Sling Lances*," on the left arm, and support with drawn Swords.*

It must be observed, as a general rule, that when the Officer commanding a Regiment, Squadron, or Division, thus marching in line, or in order of battle, or, after charging the enemy, gives the word, " *Halt*," the Lances being in the Position, " *Guard*," the whole of the Lancers will resume that of " *Carry Lances*," without waiting for that word of command.

---

* The present truly absurd and ridiculous mode of directing the front rank to make "*full waves to the front, left, and right, and to dart out the point to the front;*" and the rear rank to come to " *The St. George, with the Sword to the front*," only tends to make both men and horses unsteady in the charge : it is absolutely impossible, under such instructions, to preserve even a tolerable dressed line. A well directed charge of Cavalry should be solid, silent, and steady, like a moving wall of men and horses advancing to the attack in regular and compact order.

When the Officer commanding a Regiment, Squadron, or Division, thus marching in line, or in order of battle, wishes to gain ground on either of his flanks, or to retire, the Lances being in the Position, " *Guard,*" the whole of the Lancers will resume that of " *Carry Lances,*" at the last syllable of the preparatory order, without waiting for that word of command.

Whenever the order to " *Trot* " is intended to be given, the Lances being in the Position, " *Guard,*" the Officer commanding the Regiment, Squadron, or Division, must previously give the order to resume that of " *Carry Lances*" in order to prevent any serious or unpleasant accident.

When the Regiment, Squadron, or Division, after charging the enemy, receives the order to wheel about by threes, and to retire, the front rank, which will in such case become the rear line while retiring, will immediately, after wheeling about, bring their Lances to the Position, " *By the Right, reverse Lances,*" ready to give point to the rear, against the enemy ; and the rear rank, which will then become the front line, will immediately, on receiving the order, and before wheeling about, resume the Position " *Carry Lances,*" at the last syllable of the preparatory order, without waiting for that word of command.

When a Regiment, Squadron, or Division, thus retiring, is to be re-formed in its original order, or when any change of position or movement is about to take place, and that the Officer commanding gives the order to execute the intended manœuvre, the rear line will immediately resume the Position, " *Carry Lances*," at the last syllable of the preparatory order, without waiting for that word of command.

In all other manœuvres, or changes of position, or when it is required to break, divide, or wheel a Regiment, Squadron, or Division, in any manner whatever, when manœuvring in presence of the enemy, the Lances being in the Position, " *Guard*," the Officer commanding must previously give the order to resume that of " *Carry Lances*," by word of command.

Should a Regiment of Lancers, manœuvring in presence of the enemy, find itself placed in a difficult situation, and likely to be overpowered by superior numbers of Cavalry, the Officer commanding may give orders to form either a solid or a hollow square of Squadrons or half Squadrons, which in either case will present a front on each of the four sides to the enemy, the whole of the Lancers belonging to the front lines bringing their Lances to the horizontal Position, " *Guard*," and the rear lines coming to the usual one, the point inclined forwards, and on a line with the tops of the caps of the front rank; or the Regiment may form a close column of Squadrons, or half Squadrons, in which case, the front line will bring their Lances to the Position, "*Guard;*" the right flank to that of "*Right give Point;* the left flank to that of "*Left give Point;* and the rear line to that of "*By the Right, reverse Lances;*" the four outward sides presenting the point in every direction to the enemy, and the body of the column remaining in the Position, "*Carry Lances;*" in all of which formations, no impression or effect whatever can be made on such solid or hollow square, or close column, except by Artillery alone, provided they remain perfectly steady and unmoved ; besides which, in the latter case, should a favorable opportunity or advantage present itself, the close column is ready to deploy into line in an instant, on receiving the order.

DIVISIONS OF EXERCISE

AND

ATTACK AND DEFENCE.

PART VIII.

Divisions of Exercise.

THE Lance Exercise being combined in six Divisions of Exercise, will be practised on foot, and on horseback, according to the arrangement hereafter laid down.

The first, second, and third Divisions comprise different modes of attack and defence against Cavalry, among which, the "*Round Parry*" will be found to he particularly pre-eminent.

The fourth Division comprises the same against Infantry; and the fifth and sixth against the united attacks of both Cavalry and Infantry.

In thus arranging the six Divisions, the greatest care has been taken to vary and change the different manœuvres of the Lance, so that the Lancers are especially drilled, and thereby enabled to defend themselves in every situation in which they can be supposed to be attacked singly, by either Cavalry or Infantry, or by both united.

Each of the six Divisions is sub-divided into six different modes of attack and defence, or manœuvres, which are numbered accordingly, and marked to shew which Fleugelman the time is to be taken from.

When the Lancers have attained a sufficient degree of perfection in the Divisions of Exercise, they will be instructed to continue the succeeding manœuvres of the Divisions immediately from the positions preceding them, without returning to the " *Guard*," between the motions, or to resume the position they were previously at, according to circumstances ; and afterwards each Division may be performed singly, specifying only the particular one, according to its number, when the Lancers will take the time for each manœuvre from its respective Fleugelman ; and it must invariably be observed throughout the whole of the Divisions, that the eye follows the point in whatever direction it is given, and that the moment after the Lance is instantly withdrawn.

When the word of command, " *Reverse Lances,*" alone is given, without specifying by which side, it will always imply " *By the Right ;*" when otherwise, the word of command, " *By the Left, reverse Lances,*" will be given.

At the word, " *Attention,*" or the number of the Division being named, which should invariably precede each Division, the Lancers may be instructed to come to the Position, " *Carry Lances,*" without waiting for that word of command.

The word of command, " *Sit at Ease,*" may be given, after finishing each Division of Exercise, when the Lancers may let the Lance rest on the right shoulder, in the Position, " *Rest Lances,*" the butt being first placed in the boot or bucket attached to the off stirrup.

The Regiment, Squadron, or Division, whether on foot or on horseback, being previously told off by ranks of threes, and right and left files, and having taken and proved their distance, will then receive the preparatory word of command previous to commencing the Divisions of Exercise.

Prepare to perform Lance Exercise in Six Divisions, by Fleugelman.

AT this word of command the Lancers will remain perfectly steady and attentive, their eyes fixed to the front.

FIRST DIVISION.

Against Cavalry.

									Fleugelman.
	Carry Lances,	.	.	.	.	.			Right.
	Guard,	.	.	.	.	.			Right.
No. 1.	{ Round Parry,	.	.	.	.	.			Right.
	{ Off side, Front give Point,			.	.				Right.
2.	{ Round Parry,	.	.	.	.	.			Right.
	{ Near side, Front give Point,			.	.				Left.
3.	{ Left Parry,	.	.	.	.	.			Right.
	{ Right give Point,	.	.	.	.				Right.
4.	{ Right Parry,	.	.	.	.	.			Right.
	{ Left give Point,	.	.	.	.				Left.
5.	{ Reverse Lances,	.	.	.	.				Right.
	{ Rear give Point,	.	.	.	.				Right.
6.	{ By the Left, reverse Lances,		.	.					Right.
	{ Rear give Point,	.	.	.	.				Left.
	Guard,	.	.	.	.	.			Right.
	Carry Lances,	.	.	.	,	.			Right.

R

SECOND DIVISION.

Against Cavalry.

		Fleugelman.
	Carry Lances,	Right.
	Guard,	Right.
No. 1.	Round Parry,	Right.
	Right give Point,	Right.
2.	Round Parry,	Right.
	Left give Point,	Left.
3.	Left Parry,	Right.
	Off side, Front give Point,	Right.
4.	Right Parry,	Right.
	Near side, Front give Point,	Left.
5.	Reverse Lances,	Right.
	Rear give Point,	Right.
6.	Round Parry,	Right.
	By the Left, reverse Lances,	Right.
	Rear give Point,	Left.
	Guard,	Right.
	Carry Lances,	Right.

THIRD DIVISION.

Against Cavalry.

		Fleugelman.
	Carry Lances,	Right.
	Guard,	Right.
No. 1.	Round Parry,	Right.
	Left give Point,	Left.
2.	Round Parry,	Right.
	Right give Point,	Right.
3.	Left Parry,	Right.
	and Point,	Left.
4.	Right Parry, and Point,	Right.
5.	From the St. George, by the Left, reverse Lances,	Right.
	Rear give Point,	Left.
6.	By the Right, reverse Lances,	Left.
	Rear give Point,	Right.
	Guard,	Right.
	Carry Lances,	Right.

FOURTH DIVISION.

Against Infantry.

							Fleugelman.
	Carry Lances,	.	.	.	.		Right.
	Guard,	.	.	.	.		Right.
No. 1.	Left and Right Parry,		.	.			Right.
	Off side, Front give Point,			.	.		Right.
2.	Right and Left Parry,	.		.	.		Right.
	Near side, Front give Point,			.	.		Left.
3.	Left Parry,	.	.	.	.		Right.
	Right give Point,		.	.	.		Right.
4.	Right Parry,	.	.	.	.		Right.
	Left give Point,	.	.	.	.		Left.
5.	From the St. George, by the Left, reverse Lances,						Right.
	Rear give Point,	.	.	.	.		Left.
6.	By the Right, reverse Lances,		.	.			Left.
	Rear give Point,	.	.	.	.		Right.
	Guard,	.	.	.	.	.	Right.
	Carry Lances,	.	.	.	.		Right.

FIFTH DIVISION.

Against Cavalry and Infantry.

Fleugelman.

	Carry Lances, ...		Right.
	Guard, ...		Right.
No. 1.	Against Cavalry,	{ Left and Right Parry,	Right.
		Left give Point, .	Left.
2.	Against Infantry,	{ Right and Left Parry,	Right.
		Right give Point, .	Right.
3.	Against Cavalry,	{ Left Parry, . .	Right.
		and Point, . .	Left.
4.	Against Infantry,	{ Right Parry, . .	Right.
		and Point, . .	Right.
5.	Against Cavalry,	{ Left and Right Parry,	Right.
		Right give Point, .	Right.
6.	Against Infantry,	{ Right and Left Parry,	Right.
		Left give Point, .	Left.
	Guard, ...		Right.
	Carry Lances, ...		Right.

SIXTH DIVISION.

Against Infantry and Cavalry.

			Fleugelman.
	Carry Lances, ...		Right.
	Guard, ...		Right.
No. 1.	Against Infantry,	Left and Right Parry,	Right.
		Left give Point, .	Left.
2.	Against Cavalry,	Right and Left Parry,	Right.
		Right give Point, .	Right.
3.	Against { Infantry,	Left Parry, . .	Right.
	Cavalry,	Right give Point, .	Right.
4.	Against { Cavalry,	Right Parry, . .	Right.
	Infantry,	Left give Point, .	Left.
5.	Against { Infantry,	Right Parry, . .	Right.
	Cavalry,	Left give Point, .	Left.
6.	Against { Cavalry,	Left Parry, . .	Right.
	Infantry,	Right give Point, .	Left.
	Guard, ...		Right.
	Carry Lances, ...		Right.

After the Divisions of Exercise are performed, the Regiment, Squadron, or Division, whether on foot or on horseback, will receive orders to resume its proper formation in the following manner :

Front Form
Line or Squadron.
March.

THE right files of ranks by threes, belonging to both ranks, will stand fast. The centre and left files will advance from column, form line, and dress by the pivots.

Rear Rank,
Close Order.
March.

The rear rank will close to the front in the usual manner.

To the Centre,
Close your Files.
March.

According to order, as already laid down.

Attack and Defence.

IN preparing for the Attack and Defence,* the Lancers will be drawn up in a rank entire, or single rank, the whole armed with Lances and Sabres. After the usual preparatory words of command, they will receive orders to " *Tell off by Files, from the Right;*" the left files will then receive the word, " *By the Right, March;*" and when advanced a sufficient distance, will be ordered to " *Right About turn,*" and " *Left dress,*" while, at the same time, the right files will be directed to dress by the right, that is, both files dressing contrariwise, according to the position of the exercising ground, or the top of the riding school. Thus placed in opposed positions, they will receive orders to extend their files downwards by passage to three horses' lengths distance from each other, preparatory to circling.

The files who are to act as Swordsmen will receive the words of command, " *Left Arm, sling Lances,*" and " *Draw Swords;*" the whole will then be ordered to " *Circle Right,*" or " *Left,*" when

---

* The Pimlico instructions, in treating of the Attack and Defence, page 43, commences by remarking, that " *Much might be said on the subject, and many points and parries formed for this Exercise;*" and very *shrewdly* observes, " *That those who are* perfect *masters of their horses, will have a decided advantage over those* less *so.*" Thus ends the instruction, the rest is left to be found out either by guess-work, inspiration, or chance-medley !

the horses' shoulders will be laid in the proper direction previous to the word, "*March*," when the prescribed number will move off, and compose a certain number of circles corresponding to the size of the range, a Lancer and a Swordsman to each, or two Lancers, according to order, by which means a right and a left file will be opposed to each other in each circle. This arrangement comprises the beauty of files circling, when they keep exactly opposite to each other, right arm to right when circling in one direction, and *vice versâ* when circling the contrary one. When the antagonists have moved once or twice round the circle, to give confidence and courage to their horses, and accustom them to it, the order will be given to come to the Position, "*Guard*," when the Lancer will assume his proper one, and the Swordsman will come to that of "*Right*," (or, *Left*) *Thigh Protect*," according to the side which is vulnerable, or next his adversary. Thus prepared, the order will be given to "*Attack*," which is the signal to commence operations, when both parties will put in practice the different modes of Attack and Defence prescribed for their instruction, the Lancer parrying sometimes to the front, and at other times to the rear, on whichever side he leaves open to his antagonist, taking care to keep the point of his Lance well down, and to elevate it instantly when required, and giving point as often as an opening or an unprotected part of his adversary presents itself. The files may be turned to the "*Right*," or, "*Left About*," as often as the drill officer thinks necessary; and the men must take particular care to keep their reins tight to whichever hand they circle to, and to bend their horses in well, making them look into the circle, and close their legs to them, to support the horses, and keep them well on their haunches, bearing a double pressure on the outward leg.

General Observations.

THE Attack and Defence between a Lancer and a Hussar, or Dragoon, is a most useful practice, by giving the Lancer and the Swordsman opportunities of knowing where and how each can take advantage of the other, the Lancer particularly, by throwing up, or bearing down, his point, and, when circling, by parrying with his Lance strong across his breast. These are the chief guards against the only points or cuts that a Lancer has any occasion to fear, when opposed to a Swordsman ; and he must be most particularly attentive, and on his guard, never to allow, if possible, his antagonist to get on the rear, particularly of his right side, which I consider to be the weakest point of the Lancer. The Pimlico mode of giving point on the left rear, certainly makes that side the weakest ; but let an expert Lancer, drilled according to the instructions herein laid down, attack the best and most complete Swordsman, and he will soon convince him that the left rear is by far stronger than the right, and doubly more effective than the left rear of a Lancer giving point according to that system. A Lancer must be very indifferent indeed, who will, at any time, permit a Swordsman to close with him ; nor will he ever have the slightest chance of doing so, if he conforms to the proper instructions, keeping his Lance close and firm to the body, the right fore-arm, and the elbow, which will give him the decided advantage over the Swords-man.

The Pimlico practice, (though not entered in the Instructions,) is for the Swordsman to come to what is termed, " *The Hanging Guard*," dropping the point of the Sabre, instead of the " *Right*," (or, *Left) Thigh Protect*," on the manœuvring side. This is certainly too weak a guard to parry a Lance with the strength and effect required, whereas the uplifted Sabre, in the above two " *Protects*," will, I am confident, be found by experience to be undoubtedly the most efficient to parry the Lance and act at the same time against the Lancer, the whole force of the wrist, hand, and arm being united, and the Swordsman is thus doubly prepared for both the Attack and Defence; for if he is fortunate enough to succeed in parrying the Lance, his Sword is exactly in the proper upraised position to inflict a most decisive cut on the Lancer, or give point against him in any direction.

Though Regiments of Lancers are admirably, and equally well drilled, in the Sword Exercise, still it will be found that an expert and well instructed Lancer values his Lance far above his Sabre; and that he so well knows the decided superiority of the former arm, and the inferiority of the Sword, that when ordered to attack a highly manœuvring Lancer as a Swordsman, he will always keep his Sabre at the preparatory position for parrying, and will scarcely ever attempt to make a cut at the Lancer; in fact his whole time is thoroughly employed in parrying the Lance.

The constant practice of the Attack and Defence not only gives the Lancers confidence in the use of their Lances, but it will make them excellent horsemen, and prove to them how their hands and legs should act in unison with each other, to assist their horses; it likewise shews the breaking-in and activity of the animals. The circling should be done in a canter, and the Lances should always have balls on to prevent accidents, and the Sabres adapted for the instruction, with beviled or rounded edges, instead of being sharp, which are decidedly to be preferred to the wooden Swords now in use, which are so easily broken, and are too light and inefficient for the purpose required.

INSTRUCTION IN CLASSES,

AND

REVIEW EXERCISE.

PART IX.

Instruction in Classes.

THE whole of the Drill Instructions for the Exercise and Manœuvres of the Lance, will be communicated to each Lancer of the Squad individually ; it will, therefore, be necessary to establish three Classes into which the Lancers will be removed, according to the proficiency they make, and their expertness and dexterity in wielding the Lance.

THE first, or youngest Class, will comprise the instructions necessary for the Lance Exercise on foot, which will be divided as follows :

First Degree. THE first principles of the Exercise and Manœuvres of the Lance.

Second Degree. The opening and closing of ranks ; and taking and proving the distance of ranks and files.

Third Degree. The Lance Exercise performed in line, and in column, by word of command, and by Fleugelmen.

THE second Class will comprise the instructions and practice of the Lance Exercise on horseback.

First Degree. THE opening and closing of ranks ; taking and proving the distance of ranks and files ; and performing the Lance Exercise in line, and in column, by word of command, and by Fleugelmen.

Second Degree.   The Divisions of Exercise performed at a walk.

Third Degree.   The Divisions of Exercise performed at a gallop, and in speed.

THE third Class will comprise the general application of the whole system.

First Degree.   THE exercising range, and riding-house perfective drills; the running at the ring; the preparatory formation for circling; and for the attack and defence.

Second Degree.   The attack and defence in circles, at a canter.

Third Degree.   The attack and defence on a given right line, at a gallop, and in speed.

The regulations and instructions to be observed with respect to the drills, will be, in every respect, conformable to those fixed in His Majesty's Rules and Regulations for the Sword Exercise of the Cavalry.

Review Exercise.

AT a Review of a Regiment of Lancers, the Exercise and Manœuvres of the Lance will be performed in the following order:

1. The Six Divisions in line.

2. The Six Divisions in speed.

3. The Attack and Defence in speed.

The Six Divisions in Line.

THE Six Divisions in Line will be performed by the whole Regiment by sound of the trumpet or bugle, and by Fleugelmen; after which, the Regiment will be re-formed at close order.

The Six Divisions in Speed.

THE Six Divisions in Speed will be performed by a select Division or Detachment from each Squadron, in the following manner:

Divisions to the Front form.
March.

THE number of Divisions selected, under the command of a Subaltern or Non-commissioned Officer to each, will advance clear of the line at the sound of the trumpet or bugle, and form three horses' lengths in front of their respective Squadrons, dressing by the right.

Threes outwards wheel.
March.

The Divisions being told off by ranks of threes, and right and left files, and properly divided for each flank, and having previously received the order to come to the Position, " *Carry*," or to that of " *Trail Lances*," will conform to the movement ordained ; and upon another signal from the trumpet or bugle, and at the word, " *March*," the Divisions belonging to the right wing will wheel to the right, and those of the left, *vice versâ*, and move off at a gallop; as soon as they clear the flanks of the Regiment they will wheel inwards ; and on gaining the prescribed distance, the Commanding Officers will give the order to wheel into the new alignment, and " *Halt*," and " *Dress*," according to order."

T

Perform the Six Divisions of Exercise in speed.

The right and left file of the front rank, or the front and rear files, as may be ordered, will advance one horse's length in front of the Division, to be ready to dash forward at the sound of the trumpet or bugle; at the same time the flanks will be kept complete by passaging the remaining Lancers to the advancing flank.

First Division.

Second do.

Third do.

Fourth do.

Fifth do.

Sixth do.

Consecutively, and according to order. The advanced Lancers of each Division in speed, having their horses well in hand, will, in succession, direct their horses exactly on a given right line to the front, without deviating in the smallest degree from it, nothing being more unseemly or unsoldierly than a zig-zag line. The Lancers of the different wings, on arriving at the extremity of the range, which should comprise an extent of a hundred and fifty yards at least, will form to the rear of their opposite Divisions; by which arrangement, when the entire Six Divisions are completed, the Divisions of Lancers will have changed flanks, and will be immediately in front of each other, the officers accompanying the last file of their Divisions.

The greatest attention is necessary to regulate the Manœuvres of the Six Divisions in speed, according to the extent of ground to be galloped over, as each Division of Exercise should commence and conclude at the opposite extremities of the range.

The Attack and Defence in Speed.

THE Attack and Defence in speed will be performed by the Divisions filing successively in front, from each extremity of the range, succeeding each other at the distance of five horses' lengths, and not deviating in the smallest degree, if possible, from the given right lines; the nominated files, as Lancers and Swordsmen, attacking and defending alternately until they arrive at the opposite end of the range; after which, they will resume the Position, " *Trail Lances*," regain the rear of each flank of the Regiment at a gallop; re-join their respective Squadrons, and return to their places in line.

T 2

Conclusive Observations.

THE greatest attention possible must be paid, and the most particular and strict orders given to the Lancers, that at all times, when changing their quarters, or removing from one place to another, and when entering into, or going out of, their stables, the Lances should have balls on, or be carried with the point sufficiently elevated, at either the Position, " *Trail*," or at that of " *Shoulder*, (or, *Slope*) *Lances*," so as to clear the top of a man's and a horse's head, without endangering either; this order cannot be too severely, or too strictly, enforced, as by that means the frequent and very serious accidents will be prevented, which must otherwise inevitably occur; and the Lancers must never be permitted to carry their Lances about in a careless manner, or in a horizontal position.

In the Polish, and all other foreign services, the Lancers, as a a point of honor attached to, and due to, the Lance, invariably mount guard with them, in addition to the Sword, which has a very superior and chivalric effect, and makes the Lancers better acquainted with their arms, besides giving them an honorable attachment to the Lance. In the British service, it is singular that the Lances should be treasured up for exercise and service only; and it seems unaccountable, that modern Regiments of Lancers, like Yeomanry Cavalry, should mount guard with drawn Sabres.

Lancers, in my opinion, are either the best, or the worst, description of Cavalry employed in armies; the consequent proof of my assertion is this: a fine expert and vigorous Lancer, would, I am confident, annihilate any three experienced Dragoons or Hussars who would presume to attack him; whereas a weak and inefficient one is the most wretched of military beings, and would be sabred in an instant by a single ordinary Dragoon. To the latter, the Lance is only an incumbrance; but to the expert Lancer, it is a perfect plaything. The force of arm required to wield a Lance, can only be conceived by those who handle this formidable weapon, weighing about four pounds, and nine feet in length; it is then one must judge and acknowledge, that men, to be armed with Lances, should be most vigorous and active, and moreover possess great bodily strength, and, above all, elasticity of nerve and force of arm. The finest and strongest men should be expressly selected for Regiments of Lancers, as generally one-half of those enlisted, and the rear ranks, I have seen, are totally unfit for that duty, and can never be made expert Lancers. A Lancer should be trained solely for that service; such are the Poles, who, regarding the Lance as their national arm, are exercised, even for their amusement, in the use of it from their infancy, and exult and pride themselves upon their adroitness and dexterity in wielding the Lance. I have with rapture beheld their fine Cavalry, the Polish Lancers, when exercising, hurl their Lances to the ground, and pick them up again at full speed; however, their horses were much smaller than those of our Dragoons. The rear rank being armed with Lances, are of no use whatever, as to effect, in line as Lancers, except to fill up the chasms which may be occasionally made in the front rank in action; though for retreats, skirmishing, and attacking broken lines, and confused masses of Infantry, they are *en débandade*, equally as effective Lancers as the front rank. The Irish, I aver, will always make much finer and better Lancers than the English, as they are not bred up to the sedentary trades of the latter, but are inured to fatigue, hardships, and active duties in the open field, from their youth upwards; and the Lance (or Pike, which are synonymous terms) being likewise their national arm, they delight and pride themselves in the exercise and hurly-burly of the Lance. The Birmingham, Sheffield, and Manchester artificers will never make Lancers; the mountains of Tipperary and the wilds of Conemarra are the flowery fields for those fine fellows. Lancers would be the finest description of Cavalry for the East Indies and South America, where there are such open champaign countries, and immense extensive plains to act and manœuvre on; and in a pursuit, on the retreat of the native forces, or predatory plundering tribes, and in the armies of the Patriots, they would be found an admirable and an invulnerable arm, carrying terror throughout, for nothing can escape on a retreat, in an open country, from an expert Lancer. Lancers are just as efficient Cavalry in an enclosed country as any other description of Dragoons; and are as admirable a force to cover retreats on the high roads, as in the open country; and, from the prodigious length of the Lance when in a horizontal position, they may laugh at the attack of all other Cavalry, either in front or rear, when steady in compact line; and all Dragoons are equally as inefficient against an enemy posted behind a hedge, wall, or ditch, or in the fastnesses of a swamp. The heavy Cavalry of the British service should be practised in the Lance exercise, by having a sufficient number of Lances always in possession of each Regiment, which would give them a thorough knowledge of the merits and effect of the Lance, and instruct them how to defend themselves against Lancers hereafter, and enable them to find out their weakest points; these are the description of drills necessary to be instilled into our Cavalry, and not the inconceivable and absurd nonsense lately introduced into the British service, such as learning to cut off men's heads at a blow, parrying off wooden arms, sabring pasteboard bodies, pointing at targets, and shooting into tubs.—" *Exercet histrioniam mundus universus.*"—Scientific riding drills, running at the ring, the exercise and manœuvres of the Lance and the Sword, and active effective field days, are the grand practical exercises for the British Dragoons; and which will still keep them, as they ever have been, the admiration of Europe, and the most superior Cavalry in the world. As for the wig-blocks, wooden arms, pasteboard cuirasses, buckram suits, masks, targets, and tubs, lately introduced into Cavalry riding schools, as necessary paraphernalia for modern military riding masters, the sooner they are banished or burned, the better. The new-fashioned mode of drilling Dragoons, covered with laurels and service, to slice off men's heads *à la Turque,* is a truly indecent spectacle *in time of profound peace,* besides being ridiculous, nonsensical, and useless *at any time;* and is very aptly defined by the following burlesque descriptive alliteration, composing the sublime bathos of

WELLINGTON'S WATERLOO WARRIORS WAGING WAR AGAINST WIG-BLOCKS!!

" Spectatum admissi risum teneatis ?"

END OF THE LANCE EXERCISE.

PIMLICO DIVISIONS.

THE following three Divisions of Exercise, commonly called, " The Pimlico Divisions," comprise the Manœuvres at present practised by the four Regiments of British Lancers :

FIRST DIVISION.

AGAINST CAVALRY.

		Motions.
1st.	Guard,	1
2nd.	Front Parry and Point,	4
3rd.	Left Parry and Point,	4
4th.	Right Parry and Point,	4
5th.	Left rear Parry and Point,	4
6th.	Right rear Parry and Point,	4
7th.	Guard,	1
8th.	Carry Lance,	1

SECOND DIVISION.

AGAINST INFANTRY.

		Motions.
1st.	Guard,	1
2nd.	Right Parry and Point,	4
3rd.	Left Parry and Point,	4
4th.	Guard,	1
5th.	Reverse Lance and Rear Point,	4
6th.	Guard,	1
7th.	Port Lance and Rear Point,	4
8th.	Guard,	1
9th.	Carry Lance,	1

THIRD DIVISION.

AGAINST CAVALRY.

		Motions.
1st.	Guard,	1
2nd.	Front Wave and Point,	3
3rd.	Left Wave and Point,	3
4th.	Right Wave and Point,	3
5th.	Guard,	1
6th.	Round Parry, Port Lance, and Rear Point,	4
7th.	Round Parry, Reverse Lance, and Rear Point,	4
8th.	St. George,	1
9th.	Guard, and Carry Lance,	2

U

Comment.

THE foregoing three Divisions are literally copied from the Treatise published for the *instruction* of the British Regiments of Lancers. There is no mention whatever made of which Fleugelman the time for each motion is to be taken from ; and the whole have the word of command given in the *singular* number to a supposed plurality or body of men drawn out for exercise. What would any Regiment think of an Officer, on joining and entering into the functions of his command, and dignity of office, in all the pomp and parade of pride and power, if, by way of displaying his knowledge and improvement in the military tactique, he gave the word of command, "*Draw Sword,*" to four Squadrons, or, "*Present Arm,*" to a Battalion of Infantry, with the whole remaining words in the same remarkably *singular* key, from his *own* military treatise ? How truly extraordinary must he appear to the whole Regiment, and how ingloriously must he have retreated from the parade, and hid his deservedly diminished head, if they expressed their sense of ridicule openly, for such really could not be expected from an Officer of the Pimlico Volunteers !

Upon a comparison with the Six Divisions of Exercise formed upon the model of the inimitable Polish system, it is modestly submitted to military decision, whether a single one of those so much vaunted Pimlico productions instructs a Lancer how to defend himself if attacked by one, much less by more men, or by the united attacks of Cavalry and Infantry, in front and rear? Whether the Lancer is drilled to change his Lance quickly from one Position to another, or not? What in the annals of chivalry and romance can be more dull and heavy than Nos. 1, 2, and 3? And as for the second and third Divisions, they are a hurly-burly of nonsense beyond all understanding: for instance, after "*Left Parry and Point,*" comes "*Guard,*" and then "*Reverse Lance;*" why not change to "*Reverse Lances,*" in an instant, from the former position? And after the Point is given to the rear on the off side, whips in "*Guard*" again, and then "*Port Lance,*" (the newly baptized word for the mutilated "*Left, reverse Lances,)*" and "*Rear Point.*" Why not change from "*Right, reverse Lances*" to "*Left, reverse Lances,*" at once, without resuming the "*Guard,*" and *vice versâ?* Instead of which, when the Lancer wants to give point from the off on the near side, or from the near on the off side, he is directed to first come to the "*Guard,*" before he is to change his Lance from one position to the other. What a round-about, rigmarole manœuvre! as if it were absolutely necessary to invariably resume the "*Guard*" as an indispensable preparatory position to make every other manœuvre from. An expert Lancer, drilled according to the Polish system, would absolutely give five, nay six, or even seven parries and points, while one adhering to the puffed-off* Pimlico Instructions would give two.

* *Vide* the puffs in the Morning Post under the head of "*The Fashionable World.*"

The spear of the Lance should always be pointed to the rear in re-treating before or from an enemy, whereas, in those *celebrated instructions*, the very reverse is to be practised. How truly ridiculous, absurd, and unsoldierlike it appears at a Review, to behold an intrepid Lancer retreating with the point of his Lance turned towards his own men, instead of against his supposed enemy ; this is a complete false concord of chivalry ; not only so, but a fatal error, and a truly dangerous one ; for if the Lancer is closely pursued in such a situation, he must inevitably be cut to pieces during the pro-digious length of time he is conforming to *such* instructions ; or com-ing to the " *Guard*" alone, from any other manœuvre, without reflect-ing that he is to change from that position again, to reverse his Lance on the right or left. As for the various " *Waves and Points*," in the third Division, the words of command might just as well have been "*Whistle and Point ;*" the expression " *Wave*" being the most extraor-dinary, unmeaning, and unmilitary word ever known to have been elicited from a military brain, to be popped into the mouth of a Dragoon ; its definition (Page 29 of the Instructions) implies " *To describe the figure of eight, in order to frighten the antagonist's horse with the flag*," thereby meaning, to cabalistically inscribe that figure in the air with the point of a Lance by way of a charm, which, like the Abracadabra, that never-failing febrifuge for the ague, is supposed to have the desired effect ; this is meant, no doubt, to denote or ex-press the undulatory motion of the bandrol or flag, which, in the eternal wielding of the Lance, will always wave, whether the Lancer wishes it or not. As for the finale, "*St. George*," it gives the complete finish to the scene, by the truly absurd and highly ridiculous mode of drilling the Lancer (*Vide* Page 33 of the Instructions) to come to the " Guard," "*by throwing his Lance in the air, and catching it again, the right hand reversed*," previous to bringing it to that position; this flimsy manœuvre only disgraces a Regiment, as so many Lancers drop their Lances in the feat; and what is more risible or unsoldier-like than to see a magnanimous Lancer, after losing his Lance, wheel his horse about to ingloriously halt, and dismount to pick it up again, or to request a by-stander (as is generally the case) to be so kind as to hand him his Lance? These three paltry, insignificant, and unmilitary Divisions are the chief reasons the Lance Exercise at present practised is so universally and deservedly found fault with; and it is to be hoped that, in process of time, and for the future reputation of chivalric science, the foregoing three Divisions will be obliterated out of the page of military recollection for ever, for the credit of His Majesty's Service.

APPENDIX.

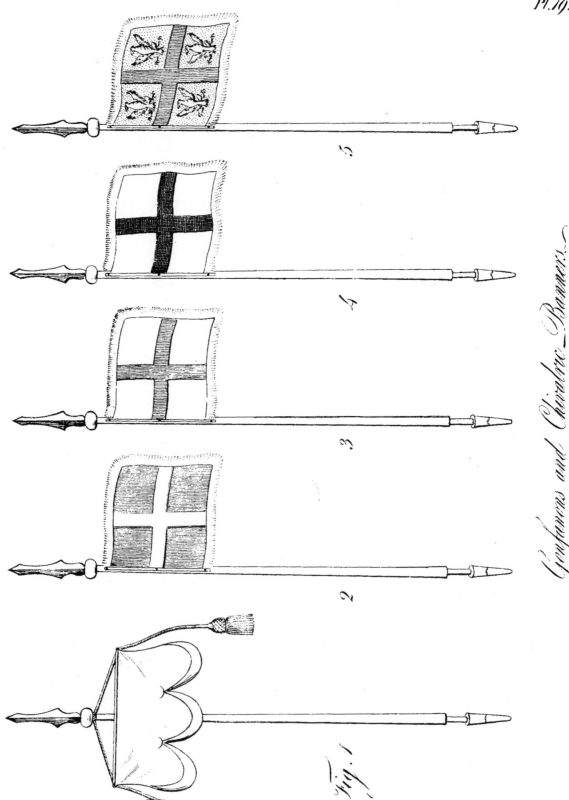

Pl. 19.

Gonfanons and Chivalric Banners.

Fig. 1.

2

3

4

5

HISTORICAL ACCOUNT

OF THE MOST

Celebrated Banners and Orders of Chivalry,

PARTICULARLY OF THE

ORIFLAMME OF ST. DENNIS,

THE BANNERS AND ORDERS OF

THE KNIGHTS OF ST. JOHN OF JERUSALEM,

(AFTERWARDS STYLED OF RHODES, AND SUBSEQUENTLY OF MALTA,)

THE KNIGHTS TEMPLARS,

THE TEUTONIC KNIGHTS OF ST. MARY OF JERUSALEM,

AND THE BANNER OF

Ancient Montmorency;

BEING EMBLEMATIC AND DESCRIPTIVE OF THE ORIGIN AND HONOR FORMERLY
ATTACHED TO BEARING GONFANONS, OR GONFALONS, AND CHIVALRIC
BANNERS, AND LANCES,

HISTORICAL ACCOUNT

OF THE MOST

CELEBRATED BANNERS AND ORDERS OF CHIVALRY.

𝔒rigin of 𝔅anners.

THE Banners and Military Ensigns, or Standards, of the different nations of the globe, present a great variety of emblems, very often singular, and almost all borrowed from religious persuasions. The Israelites had for their national ensign, the figure of an Ox's head, accompanied by two or four wings, from whence the Cherubim have been since derived. As symbols of strength, united with swiftness, these allegorical beings were supposed to draw the chariot of Thunder, on which Jehovah advanced to destroy the Heathen with his lightning. The Persians, worshippers of the Holy Fire, which preceded their armies, appear to have placed in their royal banner an image of the Sun, towards which an Eagle was darting. The Sphynx was the ensign of the Thebans; and the Owl, the sacred bird of Minerva, led the light Athenians to battle. The Goths, the Vandals, and almost all the nations who subdued the Roman empire, had for their standard a Dragon made of linen cloth, and attached to the end of a Lance. When the innumerable Cavalry of these nations advanced at full speed to the charge, the wind inflated these Dragons, they appeared to become animated, and to dart upon the enemy with hissings, like those of living serpents.

> " Hi volucres tollunt aquilas, hi picta draconum
> Colla levant, multusque tumet per nubila serpens,
> Iratus stimulant Noto vivitque receptis
> Flatibus."
>
> Claud. de 3 Honorii Consul.

> " Quid fixa draconum
> Ora velint, ventisque fluitent an vera minentur
> Sibila, suspensum rapturi faucibus hostem."
>
> Idem. de 6 Honorii Consul.

This kind of ensign, or standard, which recals to our memory the Dragon, which is the emblem of Happiness and Sovereign Power among the Chinese, may have been only an inheritance left to the nations of Europe by the Huns, who, during a period of nearly forty years, were their masters; moreover, in order to denote that the Franks will at once subdue both the Romans, and their enemies, the Visigoths, and the Burgundians, a poet of the age of Clovis thus expressed himself with great elegance:

> "Proteret Aquilam Leo Serpente collisam."
>
> Hildegast. cité par Hunnibald, chez Tritheme.

thereby signifying that, " The Eagle fights with the Dragon, but the Lion will subdue them both."

It is well known that the Romans had nothing at first for an ensign, or standard, but a bundle of hay, " *Manipulus Fœni,*" which bore reference to a custom of the Italians, of marking such bulls as were mischievous and dangerous to approach, by twisting some hay round their horns.

> " Fœnum habet in cornû, longè fuge."
>
> Hor. Sat. Lib. 1. Sat. 4, Ver. 34.

The Eagle, consecrated to Jupiter, became the ensigns of the Consular Legions, while each description of soldiers, according to the different weapons they were armed with, had likewise their peculiar standards, on which were represented the figures of horses, wild boars, minotaurs, and other animals; there were likewise, in addition to these emblems, little images of the gods, " *Numina Legionum.*" It is certain, that the standard appropriated to the Cavalry was, at least under the emperors, a narrow strip of cloth, or Bandrol of a purple colour, on which the name of the sovereign was emblazoned in letters of gold, and was called the " *Flammula.*" It was a similar standard, or sometimes a military cloak, a " *Sagum,*" attached to the end of a Lance, which, being planted before the Prætorium, announced the departure of the emperor to war.

It was, no doubt, in imitation of the sovereigns of Rome, that during the middle age, every barbarous chieftain, and afterwards every lord of a castle, or mitred prelate, had his Gonfanon, or sacred and military banner. These ensigns, without number, displayed in front of the ranks, and illumined by the sun, or agitated by the wind, gave to an army, in the age of Chivalry, a truly picturesque appearance.

> " Mille aura flante leni, vexilla subventilant."
>
> Ganfr. Malaterra, de Gestis Viscardi.

The Knights Bannerets, arrayed in all the pomp and pride of their glittering armour, were marshalled beside these, the symbols of their power; oftentimes they bore them in their hands.

> " Ni a riche homme, ni Baron
> Ki n'ait lès lui son Gonfanon,
> U Gonfanon, ou autre Enseigne,
> U in se maigne il restraigne."
>
> Rom. du Rou. cité par M. Roquefort dans
> son Glossaire de la Langue Romance.

The Oriflamme of St. Dennis.

THE Oriflamme, or Auriflamme, (Plate 19, Fig. 1.) was, as its name implies, a gilded standard, (" *Aurea Flamma.*") This is the natural etymology of the word, confirmed by William of Brittany, in his Philippide; the form, the ornaments, and the materials of this sacred banner, were, no doubt, varied according to the taste of the age. A poet of the 13th century characterizes it in the following manner:

> " Oriflambe est une Bannière,
> Aucun foi plus forte, plus guimple;
> De cendal roujoyant et simple,
> Sans pourtraicture d'autre affaire."
>
> Guillaume Guyart dans les Royaux Lignages.

The conclusion to be taken from this passage is, that the Oriflamme bore the shape of a little cope, which is not very different from that of a stomacher worn by the nuns. Cendal, or Zendalo, is, according to a manuscript note of Villoison, a By-zantine word, which has passed from Constantinople to Venice, where it still signifies a kind of veil; and it denotes likewise the cloth or silk of which those veils are made. Instead of Cendal, some authors make use of the term, " *Saint Vermeil,*" which bears reference to its colour. The Oriflamme had three pendants, or tails, and was adorned with green tufts, without gold fringe, as some have asserted, and was attached to a gilded Lance, which Raoul de Presles calls, the Glaive of the Oriflamme.

The Oriflamme is particularly celebrated in the annals and histories of France; it is therein represented as giving animation and confidence to the troops, and held sacred by them; and was only displayed as a signal that their sovereign accompanied them to battle. The Oriflamme oftentimes led them to victory; and after a defeat, those whom a victorious enemy had for an instant forced to yield to superior numbers, rallied around it, as though it were a palladium.

It is most probable that the Oriflamme, or sovereign banner of France, is only an imitation of those belonging to the Roman emperors; it must have been the same displayed by Syagrius, and after the defeat of that Roman, by Clovis. The annalists afterwards conceived it a much finer subject, to assert that it fell from heaven: they place this miracle under the reign of Clovis, when he embraced Christianity, A. D. 496; of Dagobert, A. D. 628; and of Charlemagne, A. D. 800.

Another more evident opinion considers the Oriflamme as nothing more than the Gonfanon, or sacred banner of the Abbey of St. Dennis, which was borne in the processions in honor of that saint. The Counts of Vexin, Vidames, and Avoués; that is, " Protectors of the Abbey," bore it in the private wars which the Abbey was engaged in against those who infringed upon, or usurped, their rights: it was taken from the shrine of the Holy Martyr, previous to setting out on the military expedition, and returned again, with the greatest pomp and ceremony, when it was ended; this duty was transferred, with the title, to the kings of France, under Philip the First, who united it to the crown. The kings of France, on that account, contracted the same engagements to the Abbey of St. Dennis, by virtue of which acquisition they became, as it were, feudatory to the Abbey; but were not obliged to do homage, their quality of sovereign dispensing them from this bondage. The ceremony and custom before their departure was to receive the sacred banner from the hands of the Abbot, kneeling at the same time without hood or girdle, after having previously attended High Mass at both the Churches of Nôtre Dame and St. Dennis. Sometimes the Sovereign wore the Oriflamme suspended round his neck, without displaying it in any other manner.

The ancient tradition, which bestows an Oriflamme on Clovis, and according to which testimony, this sacred Banner was principally designed for expeditions against the Infidels, comprehended under the general appellation of Saracens, is explained much more naturally according to our system. Supposing even that Charles Martel made use of the cope of St. Martin of Tours, as a Gonfanon or military banner, in the battle against Abderame, it will still be correct to give the general name of Oriflamme to this royal and consecrated Banner. Louis the Sixth was the first king of whom the French annals positively make mention as having taken the Oriflamme from the shrine of St. Dennis; it was in consequence of a war against the emperor of Germany, Henry the Fifth, who had penetrated into France, at the head of a formidable army. The Oriflamme shone afterwards at the battles of Bouvines and of Poitiers; it has been asserted that it disappeared in the year 1381, in the battle of Rosbec in Flanders, where it was borne by Peter de Villiers, lord of l'Isle Adam; but it afterwards was known to have been displayed again. William Martel is the last lord who was charged with the defence of the Oriflamme, in the year 1414, against the English; but he was slain the next year at the battle of Azincourt or Agincourt: there, for the last time, this celebrated banner appeared in the French armies; nevertheless, a manuscript chronicle asserts, that Louis the Eleventh took the Oriflamme from the shrine of St. Dennis, and displayed it in 1465; but the historians of that period are silent on this subject. There is mention again made of the Oriflamme in two Inventories of the Treasure of the Abbey of St. Dennis, written in the years 1534 and 1594. The following, according to Du Cange, are the terms of those particular Inventories:

"Etendart d'un cendal fort épais, fendû par le milieu, en façon d'un Gonfanon fort caduque, enveloppé antour d'un Baton couvert de cuivre doré, et un fer longuet, aigû au bout."

Du Cange Dissert. 18me. sur l'Histoire de St. Louis.
Comp. Galland. Traité de l'Oriflamme.

"A Standard of very thick cloth, divided in the middle, in the form of a Gonfanon, or sacred banner, very much decayed, wrapped round a staff mounted with gilded brass, and a long iron spear, sharp at the point."

THE

𝕭anner and 𝕺rder of the 𝕶nights of 𝕸alta.

THE first Crusade to the Holy Land was brought about by the celebrated Peter the Hermit, A. D. 1093, who, animated by holy zeal, embarked at Jaffa, came to Rome, addressed himself to the then reigning Pope, (Urban the II.,) and afterwards, by his command, visited the different courts of Europe, to prevail upon the sovereign princes to take an active part in the re-conquest of Palestine; and having succeeded in his mission, two grand councils were held previous to the assembling of the expedition, one at Plaisance in Italy, and the other at Clermont in Auvergne, A. D. 1095; at the latter of which, after a most impressive and eloquent oration from the Pope, the whole assembly rose up of one accord, and exclaimed, "*Dieu le veut,*" "*God wills it,*" which three memorable words afterwards became the renowned motto, or *Cri de Guerre* of the Crusaders, who, at the commencement, were distinguished by nothing more than a red Cross on the right shoulder.

The principal noblemen who held the chief commands in the first Crusade were, the famous Boemond, son of Robert Guiscard, Duke of Calabria; Godfrey de Bouillon, Duke of Brabant, with his brothers Eustace and Baldwin; Reymond de St. Gilles, Count of Thoulouse; Hugh de Vermandois, surnamed the Great, brother of Philip the First, King of France; Robert, Duke of Normandy, brother of William Rufus, King of England; Robert, Count of Flanders; Stephen, Count of Chartres and Blois; Alberic de Montmorency; Baldwin de Burgh; Tancred de Hauteville, nephew of Boemond; Counts Ranulp and Richard, his cousins; Hermand de Cani; Robert de Sourdeval, and a considerable number more of the nobility and gentry of France, who absolutely sold their lands, castles, and patrimony, to furnish the expenses of this famed expedition.

The general rendezvous of the first Crusade was in the plains of Constantinople; the Crusaders arrived successively from the different parts of Europe, and finally amounted to 100,000 Cavalry and 600,000 Infantry; among which were a confused medley of priests and monks, together with an inconceivable number of women habited in male attire, who, in order not to be separated from their lovers, and those they held most dear, accompanied the expedition; and in the second Crusade, in which more than 200,000 men perished, under Louis the Seventh, A. D. 1147, according to Robert de Monte, the women were absolutely reviewed, mounted and armed like Amazons, and formed several squadrons, under the command of Eleanor his queen, who accompanied them to the Holy Land. The first Crusade was finally reviewed in the plains of Constantinople by Alexis Comnène, Emperor of the East, A. D. 1096, who, after the conquest of Nicea, gained by their valour alone, became jealous of their power, betrayed them, and entered into a league with Solyman, Caliph of Egypt, against the Crusaders. They afterwards, under Boemond, conquered Natolia and Cilicia, captured Antioch, and finally arrived before Jerusalem on the 7th of June, A.D. 1099, with only 1,500 effective Cavalry, and 20,000 Infantry remaining out of the 700,000 men who had left Europe, the remainder having perished either in battle, by disease, and desertion, or were left to garrison their conquests. The city of Jerusalem was taken on the

15th of July following, after a siege of only five weeks; the slaughter was immense, more than 10,000 of the inhabitants were massacred even after they surrendered; the very children were butchered in the arms of, and at their mothers' breasts; and after the conquerors were glutted with vengeance and cruelty, they marched bare-footed, in token of humiliation, to, and prostrated themselves in the most religious manner before, the Holy Sepulchre. Shortly after they resolved on the mode of government to be adopted, and, finally, elected Godfrey de Bouillon as their king; but, at the ceremony of his intended coronation, he refused that august rank, and the crown of gold offered to him, protesting against receiving such an honor in a city where the Saviour of the world was crowned with thorns; and he modestly assumed, as his title, the Defender of the Holy Sepulchre.

Godfrey de Bouillon, on entering into power, visited the Hospital of St. John, originally founded in the Eleventh Century, by nothing more or less than a company of Italian merchants, as an asylum for the pilgrims on their arrival at Jerusalem, against the insults of the Mahometans and schismatic Greeks. A considerable number of the Crusaders immediately entered into, and adopted the regular habit of, the Hospitallers; which, at the commencement, consisted merely of a simple black robe, on which was attached, on the left side, next the heart, a plain white Cross with eight points.

The Hospitallers founded the magnificent temple of St. John the Baptist, A. D. 1100; and from the immense wealth which flowed into their possession from the liberality of the christian princes, they also established and endowed great hospitals, as receiving houses, in all the principal maritime provinces of Europe, as rendezvous for the pilgrims who devoted themselves to visit the Holy Land; such were the establishments of St. Giles in Provence, of Seville in Andalusia, of Tarentum in Apulia, of Messina in Sicily, and a great number of others: these were the first Commanderies belonging to the order, which Pope Paschal the Second afterwards took under the special protection of the Church, and which his successors honored with particular privileges.

It was not until the year 1118, under Baldwin, who succeeded his brother Godfrey de Bouillon, and took the title of First King of Jerusalem, which the other refused, that the Hospitallers elected a Grand Master, being before governed by Gerard de Provence, their founder; the first Grand Master was Raimond Dupuy, of the Province of Dauphiny; he resolved to raise among the Hospitallers a military corps, to establish a perpetual Crusade, subject to the orders of the King of Jerusalem, whose grand and solemn profession of faith was to wage an eternal war against the Infidels; he therefore divided the Hospitallers into three classes, the first of which was purely military, and comprised the Knights; the second the ecclesiastical department; and the third those who, having no pretensions to nobility, but whose office it was to attend the sick in the hospitals, were designated by the style of the Administering Brothers, or "*Frerès servans;*" this last class was afterwards distinguished, by order of Pope Alexander the Fourth, by a different Cross, from the Knights of St. John of Jerusalem.

The new religious and military Order increased surprizingly in number and in riches; and was sub-divided into seven divisions, termed "*Langues,*" viz. Of Provence, Auvergne, France, Italy, Arragon, Germany, and England; but the latter was struck out of the Order on the establishment of the Protestant religion in that country; and to that of Arragon was afterwards attached those of Castile and of Portugal.

The military Banner of the celebrated religious and military Order of the Knights Hospitallers of St. John of Jerusalem, afterwards styled, of Rhodes, and subsequently, of Malta, (Plate 19, Fig. 2,) was composed of a white or silver *(argent)* full Cross, on a golden *(or)* field; this heraldic escutcheon, or armorial bearings, the Knights also, by order of Pope Alexander the Fourth, wore embroidered on their Sopraveste, or Surcoat, on the left side, next the heart, together with the enamelled Cross of the Order, to distinguish them from those who administered relief to the sick in the hospitals, and who were not militarily armed; these wore the regular habit, consisting of a black robe with a pointed cloak, which was styled the "*Manteau à bec,*" and to which was likewise attached a Capuchin's hood of the same colour: they also bore, on the left side, next the heart, the original plain white linen Cross, with eight points; the dress of the sisters of the Order differed from those of the Hospitallers, being a scarlet robe with a black cloak, and to which was likewise attached the same white linen Cross, with eight points.

The heroic valour and honorable devotion of those justly celebrated Knights, has long since in after ages made their Order highly distinguished in the historic page; their very eminent achievements at the sieges of Jerusalem, Jaffa, Tyre, Ascalon, Acre, Damietta, throughout all Egypt, and at the capture of Rhodes, and their defence of Malta, and the constant and bloody wars they nobly sustained against the Infidels, fully entitled them to the truly exalted and very conspicuous part they bear in the annals of chivalry. The historian of the siege of Acre, A. D. 1190, in treating of their determined bravery under the Duke of Suabia, son of Frederick the First, Emperor of the East, at this memorable siege, thus describes them in curious rhyme:

" Hospitales milites ab equis descendunt,
Ut ursa pro filiis, cum Turcis contendunt,
Turcis nostrum aggerem per vim bis conscendunt,
Hos sagittis sauciant, hos igne succendunt,
Et Hospitalarii equos ascenderunt,
Et Turcos à latere maris invaserunt,
Quos ad urbis mœnia per vim reduxerunt,
Et ex his in foveis multos occiderunt.

> Monachi Florentini, Iconensis Episcopi, de recuperatâ Ptolemaïde.

The Knights of St. John of Jerusalem were driven out of the Holy Land, together with the Knights Templars and Teutonic Knights, under their Grand Master, John de Villiers, by Melech Seraf, Soldan of Egypt, A. D. 1291; established their Order afterwards at Rhodes; and on their expulsion from that island, under their Grand Master, Philip de Villiers de l'Isle Adam, by the Emperor Solyman the Second, A. D. 1522, they finally fixed themselves at Malta, which was granted to them by the Emperor Charles the Fifth, by a donation signed the 24th of March, A. D. 1530, from whence they derived their latest appellation.

The island of Malta was surprized and conquered, after a very feeble resistance, by Napoleon Buonaparte, in his expedition to Egypt, on the 11th of July, 1798; re-taken by the British, A. D. 1800; agreed afterwards to be returned to the Order by the treaty of Amiens, signed the 27th of March, 1802; but which surrender was refused to be ratified, without the stipulations being carried into effect. The Knights, at this present period, after establishing a seat for the Order in Calabria, under their Grand Master, Thomasi, are chiefly dispersed throughout Europe, their property either confiscated or withheld from them, and the island of Malta formally ceded to, and garrisoned by, Great Britain.

THE

Banner and Order of the Knights Templars.

THE once powerful, celebrated, finally unfortunate and persecuted, religious and military Order of the Knights Templars, was instituted A. D. 1128, and derived its origin, according to William of Tyre, from nothing more than a simple association of Noblemen, consisting of Hugh de Payens, Geoffrey de St. Aldemar, and seven more of the French nobility, whose names are unknown: they formed among themselves a small military band, or armed association, to serve as an escort to the pilgrims on their arrival in the Holy Land, to conduct them safe to Jerusalem, through the dangerous passes and defiles of the mountains. The English historian, Brompton, describes them as elèves of the Knights of St. John of Jerusalem, and who subsisted at first by their bounty alone. According to William of Tyre, they inhabited a pavilion close to the Temple of Jerusalem, from which they derived their appellation of Templars, or Knights of the Temple. Baldwin, King of Jerusalem, having sent Hugh de Payens on a mission to Rome to solicit Pope Honorius the Second to interest himself with the sovereigns of Europe for the formation of a new Crusade; this pious Nobleman, on presenting his companions, recounted to him the zeal of the Templars in behalf of the pilgrims, and demanded his permission to found a new religious and military Order, similar to the Knights of St. John of Jerusalem, which was immediately granted, their institution approved of at the council of Troyes, and himself nominated the first Grand Master of the Knights Templars. The truly ridiculous statutes and formalities exacted from this Order by St. Bernard, who assisted at the council, were, that they should repeat a certain number of Paters each day, by which, it is to be presumed, they did not know how to read; likewise, that they should eat flesh meat only three days in the week, but were permitted to be served on fast days with three dishes of other food.

This new religious and military Order immediately increased to a surprising degree, and became, in process of time, numerous, rich, and powerful. Sovereign princes, and the most illustrious of the nobility entered it; and as the Knights Templars made no vows to attend the poor and the sick in the hospitals, they were particularly joined by persons of the most exalted rank and highest distinction. Brompton, the English historian, particularly mentions, that they even eclipsed by far, and were preferred to the Knights of St. John of Jerusalem.

" Hi namque, secundum quosdam, ex infimis Hospitalariorum congregati, et ex reliquiis eorum, ex cibis et armis sustentati, ad tantum rerum opulentiam devenerunt, ut filia ditata matrem suffocare et supergredi videretur."

Chronicon. Joan. Brompton. Hist. Anglic. p. 1008, Lond. 1652.

The military banner of the Knights Templars, (Plate 19, Fig. 3,) was composed of a red *(gules)* full Cross, on a white *(argent)* field ; this heraldic escutcheon, or armorial bearings, the Knights, in imitation of those of St. John of Jerusalem, by order of Pope Eugene the Third, wore embroidered on their Sopraveste, or Surcoat, on the left side, next the heart, together with the enamelled Cross of the Order; their dress was appointed to be white, as a symbol of their profession ; they were allowed an esquire and three horses each; but all superfluous ornaments and gilded trappings were most strictly forbidden in their accoutrements and equipments.

The celebrated Reymond Berenger, Count of Barcelona, entered this highly favored Order, though at an advanced period of life; and Alphonso, King of Navarre and Arragon, absolutely made them his heirs, together with the Knights of St. John of Jerusalem, and of the Holy Sepulchre ; but which testament was afterwards over-ruled and set aside by the Grandees of these kingdoms, who asserted that Alphonso had it not in his power to dispose of his kingdoms to the prejudice of his lawful heir, and the natural right of his people, in default of an heir, to elect their own Sovereign. Conditions were afterwards stipulated and entered into relative to the inheritance : immense portions of lands, and other property, together with one-tenth of the tributes of these kingdoms were assigned to the Knights ; and the lawful heir of Alphonso, his brother Don Ramiro, succeeded to the throne.

The Knights Templars particularly distinguished themselves at Gaza, Jerusalem, and Ascalon ; they were almost all massacred, or taken prisoners, together with the Knights of St. John of Jerusalem, according to Hoveden, at the battle of the Tiberiad, A. D. 1187, by Saladin, Sultan of Egypt, owing to the treachery of the Count de Tripoli, in which action the true Cross was taken by the Infidels, and never returned afterwards. They signalized themselves in the noblest manner at the memorable siege, of Acre, which was captured under Richard Cœur de Lion of England, on the 13th July, A. D. 1191; and afterwards purchased the Isle of Cyprus from Richard for 300,000 livres, but were obliged to abandon it, and return it to the King of England on account of their tyranny and oppression; and the historians of these times relate, that Richard Cœur de Lion, before quitting the Holy Land, captured Jaffa and Ascalon, and made an extraordinary truce with the Infidels, which was to last three years, three months, three weeks, three days, three hours, and three minutes. According to Matthew Paris, the Knights Templars, those of St. John of Jerusalem, and the Teutonic Knights, nearly all perished, or were made prisoners in a battle close to Jerusalem, A. D. 1243, against the Corasmins, a tribe of Barbarians who were driven out of Persia by Keiouc or Tuly, one of the sons of the celebrated Gengis Khan, who succeeded to that kingdom; and at this memorable battle there escaped only sixteen of the Knights of St. John of Jerusalem, thirty-three Knights Templars, and three Teutonic Knights, and both the Grand Masters of the two first Orders were killed at the head of their Knights; but from the great avidity of those entering the different Orders to immediately join their ranks, they were soon recruited again. Several divisions, at different periods, arose from ancient animosity and jealousy between the Knights of St. John of Jerusalem and the Templars; and, A. D. 1254, the two Orders came to a general engagement; the combat was for a long time doubtful, until at length the Knights of St. John triumphed; and, as the Templars refused quarter, scarcely one remained alive to announce the news of their defeat; the Orders, however, became reconciled afterwards; and at the last siege of Acre, A. D. 1291, by the Sultan Melech Seraf, the Grand Master of the Templars, Peter de Beaujeu was elected commandant, where he was killed, and the few Knights of his Order who escaped, on the evacuation of the Holy Land, accompanied those of St. John of Jerusalem to Limisso in the island of Cyprus, which the Templars abandoned A. D. 1308, by order of the Pope, under their last Grand Master, James de Mola, and dispersed themselves throughout France, and the different christian states where their rich Commanderies were situated.

The Knights Templars have been accused of having offered their services to Pope Boniface the Eighth, against Philip le Bel, King of France, A. D. 1301; and also to have furnished him with considerable sums of money to commence a war against him, which induced Philip, out of revenge, to oblige Pope Clement the Fifth to afterwards take measures for the entire abolition and consequent extinction of the Order; there was also a great comparison made, at this period, between the conduct of the Knights of

St. John and the Templars, on account of the former remaining in the East, and capturing the island of Rhodes on the 15th of August, A. D. 1310, which was not in the least to the advantage of the Templars. It appeared as if the Order of St. John never gave up the hopes of driving the Infidels out of the Holy Land, by their still remaining in the East, and occupying the port of Rhodes as a grand rendezvous for the Crusades, while the Templars, by their precipitate retreat into their rich Commanderies in Europe, and by the loose, dissipated, and effeminate life they led, which occasioned the ancient proverb of, " *Boire comme un Templier,*" " *To drink like a Templar ;*" appeared to have renounced their sacred vocation, and left the Holy Land a prey to the Turks and Saracens ; this, and the revenge which the King of France owed them, paved the way to the total extirpation of their Order.

The precise year is not known when Philip le Bel formed the terrible resolution to abolish this once powerful and celebrated Order. Historians say, that two Templars being accused of enormous crimes and impiety, and condemned to death by the Grand Master, one of them, out of revenge, and knowing Philip's determination to destroy the Order, refused to confess except to the king alone, upon which Philip expressly came to Paris; and the Templar being promised a pardon, and even a recompense, if he declared the truth, he accused the whole Order of theft, homicide, idolatry, and the most infamous crimes; he added, that the grand secret of the Templars, on their initiation, was, to renounce Jesus Christ, and as a sign of detestation of his name, to spit on the Cross; that the whole of the Order became privately Mahometans; and, by the most infamous treason, had sold the Holy Land to the Sultan of the Infidels.

Philip recounted all these accusations to the Pope, at Lyons; and the following year, in a more ardent manner at Poitiers; but the Pope, by delays and excuses, put him off, with the hope that time and circumstances would induce the king to alter his intentions ; but at last he became impatient of the delay of the Pope, and, by a secret order, arrested in one day (the 13th of October, 1307) the Grand Master, and all the Knights Templars in Paris, and throughout France: he also seized upon the whole of their property, which was placed at the disposal of the crown.

Clement the Fifth, on hearing of the imprisonment of the Grand Master, and the Templars, affected great indignation and resentment at first; and endeavoured, by his authority, to suspend the powers of those who were to try them : he wrote himself to the king, demanding the persons and property of the Templars, which, after some hesitation, was finally acceded to, though they were always guarded by the subjects of Philip, who, to deceive and appease the Pope, plausibly gave for his excuse, that they were guarded in his name and that of the church. Their trial, at length, commenced, and all those who did not acknowledge themselves guilty, were put to the severest torture: the cries and groans of the Knights, whose limbs were almost torn asunder, resounded throughout the prisons: a considerable number, to escape the torture, avowed every thing required of them; but a far greater, in the middle of their torments, asserted their innocence with the most exalted firmness, and even invincible obstinacy. The Pope gave orders that the Grand Master, and the chief officers of the Order should be conducted to Chinon; and it is pretended, that the former, and seventy-two Knights, confessed all the crimes imputed to them; but afterwards, both the Grand Master, and the greater part of these Templars openly declared, that their confessions of guilt were extorted from them by torture, and they denied the whole.

During this persecution the whole of the Christian Princes of Europe arrested all the Templars throughout their states, seized upon their property, and placed garrisons in their Commanderies. Two grand councils were held at Vienne in Dauphiny, the first on the 16th of October, A.D. 1311, and the second on the 22nd of May, A.D. 1312, at which Pope Clement the Fifth, in the most solemn manner, completely broke, annulled, and abolished the entire religious and military Order of the Knights Templars. The Grand Master, James de Mola, was brought back to Paris: the Knights who had confessed themselves guilty on their trials, were obliged, as a mark of the horror with which they regarded their late Order, to leave off the dress of the Knights Templars, and to shave their long beards, which they wore according to the custom of the East. Those who persisted in their protestations of innocence were treated with the utmost severity; fifty-four of the Knights were burned alive by a slow fire, without the Porte St. Antoine at Paris, A.D. 1312, though offered a general pardon by the king if they would confess themselves guilty, which the whole refused; and an immense number more were burned alive in the same manner throughout the kingdom.

The following year A.D. 1313, after the dissolution of the Order, it was resolved to finish this infamous tragedy, and to decide upon the fate of the Grand Master, James de Mola, and the three principal officers of the Order, Guy de Viennois, Hugh de Peralde, Grand Prior of France, and the Grand Prior of Aquitaine: they were led out upon a scaffold in the square of the Cathedral of Nôtre Dame at Paris, with the hope of their confessing their guilt before the people, for which they were promised a

z

general amnesty, while, on the other side, a pile of wood was erected to burn them alive, if they persisted in their innocence. Hugh de Peralde, and the Grand Prior of Aquitaine, at the sight of so dreadful a punishment, acknowledged themselves guilty; but the Grand Master, shaking the chains he was loaded with, advanced to the edge of the scaffold, and asserted his innocence with a loud voice, and in the most eloquent manner. Guy de Viennois came afterwards, and made a like oration, solemnly declaring the innocence of the entire Order, on which, the whole four were obliged to descend the scaffold, and were remanded to prison. Philip, naturally vindictive, and actuated solely by avarice and revenge, gave instant orders that the Grand Master and Guy de Viennois should be burned alive at a slow fire that same day, A. D. 1313, which was rigorously executed on the exact spot, in the little island of the Seine, close to the Pont Neuf at Paris, where the new statue of Henry the Fourth is now erected. The Grand Master, in the midst of his torments, protested his innocence, but avowed he deserved death for having once confessed himself guilty, though extorted from him by torture; and it is confidently related, that when surrounded by flame and smoke, and tied to a stake, he was heard to exclaim with a loud voice, "Clement, unjust judge and cruel executioner, I cite thee to appear before the tribunal of God in forty days, and thou, Philip, in one year;" perhaps the fact of the Pope and the King dying at these exact periods, gave rise to this rumour. The ashes of the victims were collected by the people as holy relics. The Grand Priors of France and Aquitaine ended their days in prison; though according to Paulus Emilius, one of them was burned alive with James de Mola and Guy de Viennois: and the two apostate Knights, the authors of this frightful catastrophe, ended their lives in a most wretched manner, one being hung for new crimes, and the other assassinated. With regard to the property and riches of this unfortunate Order, the greater part was assigned to the Knights of St. John of Jerusalem, except that situated in Spain, which was reserved to be applied to the expulsion of the Moors from that kingdom. The possessions situated in Germany were adjudged to the Teutonic Knights, but the money and moveable effects were divided among the Pope and the different sovereigns of the states their Commanderies were in, who profited particularly by the wreck and the spoils of the Order. The King of Portugal, however, made use of an honorable pretext to prevent the Knights of St. John of Jerusalem from succeeding to their property in his kingdom, by instituting the Order of Christ, to which he annexed the possessions formerly belonging to the Knights Templars; and which grant was afterwards confirmed by Pope John the Twenty-second, at his solicitation, to this new Order of Chivalry.

THE

𝕭anner and 𝕺rder of the 𝕿eutonic 𝕶nights.

THE religious and military Order of the Teutonic Knights of St. Mary of Jerusalem was instituted A. D. 1190, and entirely confined to the German nation, none other being admitted; they were originally nothing more than a society of from forty to fifty Germans, from the towns of Bremen and Lubec, who followed the Knights of St. John of Jerusalem to the Holy Land, to attend the sick of their own nation in the hospitals, and to administer relief to those who stood in need of succour and assistance: from such a comparative small beginning this noble society insensibly formed a new Order of Chivalry, imitating the example of the Knights of St. John of Jerusalem, and the Knights Templars, which, in process of time, obtained the rights of sovereignty in Europe, after having conquered Prussia.

The title of Teutonic, attached to the Order, derives its appellation from Teuta or Tuisco, the most ancient or peculiar idol, or rather deified great ancestor of the Teutones, or ancient Germans and Saxons, the reputed son of Mercury. Aventinus describes Tuisco as the son of Noah, who was sent by his father into Germany 131 years after the general deluge; but with more probability, he was the son of Ascenas, great grandson of Noah, and grandson of Japhet, who settled in Germany, and was worshipped after his decease by all his posterity. According to Verstegan, Tuesday derives its appellation from Tuisco. The modern Germans nearly preserve their former name, being by ancient geographers called "𝕮uptsch," or "𝕯uptsch," and by the present "𝕮eutsch," or "𝕯eutsch," or Dutch people, and the whole country "𝕮eutschland," or "𝕯eutschland." The Italians style a German waltz, "*Danza tedesca.*"

Pope Celestine the Third, at the particular request of the emperor of Germany, (Henry the Sixth,) solemnly approved of, and confirmed the institution of the Teutonic Knights on the 23rd of February, A. D. 1192; their vows were exactly the same as those of the Knights of St. John of Jerusalem, and the Knights Templars, and they observed the regulations of the former, as to attending the sick in the hospitals, and of the latter, in their military discipline: the epithet of St. Mary of Jerusalem was bestowed on them, on account of their hospital being dedicated to the Virgin Mary, whence they were likewise styled, " *Marian Knights.*"

The military banner of the Teutonic Knights of St. Mary of Jerusalem, (Plate 19, Fig. 4,) was composed of a black *(sable)* full cross, on a white *(argent)* field : this heraldic escutcheon, or armorial bearings, the Knights also wore embroidered on their Sopraveste, or Surcoat, on the left side, next the heart, together with the enamelled Cross of the Order ; their dress was appointed to be white, like the Knights Templars : and those who administered relief to the sick in the hospitals, and were not militarily armed, wore a regular habit and hood, similar in shape to those of the Hospitallers of St. John, to which was likewise attached a plain black full linen cross, on the left side, next the heart. Those three religious and military Orders were the generous defenders of the Holy Land, and to them was very appropriately applied, in former ages, the following sacred lines :

" Τὸ σπαρτιον τὸ ἐντριτον οὐ ταχεως ἀποῤῥαγήσεται."

" Filum triplicatum non cito abrumpitur."

Ecclesiastes, Cap. 4, Ver. 12.

The Teutonic Knights, after eminently distinguishing themselves in the Holy Land, chiefly emigrated to Prussia under their Grand Master, Herman de Saltza, A. D. 1226, by the invitation of Conrad, Duke of Suabia, where they shortly acquired, by conquest, almost the entire of that country, the inhabitants of which were then Pagans, and who were almost totally extirpated by those religious Knights, who undertook their conversion by the edge of the sword : the remainder of the Order followed them into Prussia, after the expulsion of the Christians from the Holy Land, A. D. 1291, where they enjoyed the rights of sovereignty for a considerable period, and became one of the most eminent Orders in Europe ; but on account of their internal divisions, they, in after ages, lost both their power and possessions ; and Albert, Duke of Brandenburg, A. D. 1525, on abjuring Popery, abdicated the Grand Mastership, subdued all Prussia, and expelled the whole of the Papists who did not follow his example. Thus ended the sovereignty of the Teutonic Order, after it had subsisted 300 years.

The Teutonic Order is now divided into two branches, and a Grand Master is still kept up in Germany : the Protestants have their chief seat at Utrecht, and that for the Catholics is at Mergentheim, or Mariendal, of which the members take the oath of celibacy: the badge of the Order is now worn round the neck with a gold chain.

The Elector Frederic William of Brandenburgh, deservedly styled the Great, had Ducal Prussia, in addition, conferred on him A. D. 1657, and his descendants were declared independent and sovereign lords also of that part of the kingdom; afterwards his son Frederic was raised to the title of king, and proclaimed January 18th, A. D. 1701, whose posterity now enjoy the sovereignty of all Prussia.

The Banner of Ancient Montmorency.

THE military banner of the most ancient and illustrious house of Montmorency, (Plate 19, Fig. 5,) was originally composed of a red *(gules)* full cross, on a golden *(or)* field. Bouchard (the first) de Montmorency, one of the chief lords of France, under Lothaire, signalized himself by his extraordinary valour in the wars of that reign, and particularly against Otho the Second, emperor of Germany, who had entered France at the head of an army consisting of 60,000 men, A. D. 974, in order to revenge himself against Lothaire, who had conquered and deprived him of Upper Lorraine; Otho advanced towards Paris, spreading death and dismay throughout the country; he attacked and carried the castle of Montmorency by assault; Paris would have shared the same fate, had it not been for the noble courage of Geoffrey, Count of Anjou, surnamed Grisegonelle, on account of his wearing a grey tunic over his armour: this hero, a near relation of Bouchard's, defended Paris with such obstinacy, that he gave a sufficient time to Lothaire to join him with a very considerable force.

Otho, astonished at the activity, courage, concert, and threats of the French, whom he had reckoned on surprizing, fled, after having destroyed the ancient castle of Montmorency; but his precipitate retreat did not, however, save him from a most signal, ignominious, and bloody defeat. Lothaire, the bravest of the descendants of Charlemagne, came up with his army at the passage of the river Aisne, near Soissons, and first completely defeated his rear guard, and then totally annibilated his entire army. Bouchard de Montmorency, who had his own private injuries to avenge, distinguished himself above all in this memorable battle; he advanced to the charge, and attacked the enemy with, and under the auspicies of, his very propitious *Cri de Guerre*, " *Dieu ayde*," (the present motto belonging to the ancient armorial bearings, derived from the obsolete " *Diex aye*," the celebrated war-cry of the Normans in former ages,) and captured four standards, or imperial eagles, from the emperor; in memory of this renowned achievement, he, by order of Lothaire, adorned the red cross on his banner with four eagles, one in each quarter, as delineated thereon, and which still continues to be the armorial bearings of the branch of the Montmorencys of England and Ireland, his descendants, as derived from Geoffrey, the second son of Hervey de Montmorency, Grand Butler of France, who accompanied William the Conqueror into England A. D. 1066, Robert (Fitzstephen) and Hervey de Montmorency, chief constable of all Ireland, styled also de Montemarisco, and Mountmorrës, in ancient and modern history, the conquerors of Ireland, under the renowned Richard de Clare, surnamed Strongbow, Earl of Pembroke, A. D. 1169, and 1172, and Geoffrey, thrice Viceroy of Ireland, A. D. 1215 to 1234, the ancient Barons de Marisco and de Montemarisco.

From a strange coincidence of events, the Emperor Otho the Fourth entered Flanders at the head of an army consisting of 150,000 men, A. D. 1214. Philip Augustus, King of France, displaying the Oriflamme, marched against him with only 50,000 men; the great inequality of his force did not, however, prevent him from giving battle to the emperor; the two armies engaged in the plains of Bouvines, celebrated on account of the most glorious, important, and decisive victory ever gained by the French. Matthew (the second) de Montmorency, contributed particularly to obtaining the victory, and fought on that very memorable day in the most signal manner: he commanded the right wing with the Duke of Burgundy and the Count de Beaumont, which at the onset cut 2,000 Flemish Gensd'armes to pieces, when perceiving that the Count of Flanders, the bravest of the enemy's generals, was on the point of falling on that part of the army commanded by the king in person, he flew to his assistance, and performed prodigies of valour: it was in this part of the conflict the most blood was shed; the Duke of Burgundy had his horse killed under him, and while his knights were re-mounting him, Matthew de Montmorency, mounted on his charger, with his sabre in his hand, fought like a common soldier, and turned the fate of the day; he captured twelve standards, or imperial eagles, from Otho the Fourth, in the same heroic manner that his ancestor Bouchard took four from Otho the Second; the French, animated by his example, made great efforts; the Imperialists and Flemish were completely overthrown and put to flight, leaving 30,000 dead on the field of battle. Philip Augustus, by the signal and distinguished conduct of Matthew de Montmorency, acquired the greatest glory, for never was a defeat more complete, or more decisive. To commemorate the brilliant achievement of Matthew de Montmorency, who was the chief means of his obtaining the victory, and contributing to his triumph, he ordered him to add the twelve imperial eagles he had gained by his valour, to the four already borne on his banner; and which sixteen, four in each quarter, with the original red cross, on a golden field, together with the motto, " *Dieu ayde au premier Baron chretien*," constitute, at this present day, the armorial bearings of the branch of the Montmorencys of France, his descendants.

> " Pérque faces numerantur avi, sempérque renata
> Nobilitate virent, et prolem fata sequuntur,
> Continuum simili servantia lege tenorem."
>
> Claudian.

THE END.